the key to english

TWO-WORD VERBS

the key to english

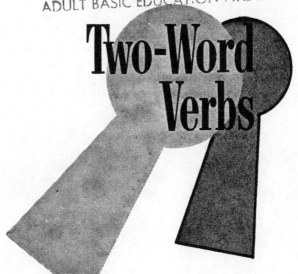

Two-Word Verbs

MACMILLIAN PUBLISHING CO., INC.
New York
COLLIER MACMILLAN PUBLISHERS
London

Macmillan Publishing Co., Inc.
866 Third Avenue, New York, N.Y. 10022

Collier Macmillian Canada, Inc.
Printed in the United States of America

ISBN 0-02-971720-5

20 19 18

PREFACE

This manual is intended to help the student, either in a class or working alone, to master a troublesome matter in English verb patterning, namely, the combination VERB + ADVERB (or PREPOSITION), with or without a following noun object. These combinations are variously called "two-word verbs" (as in this book), "merged verbs," "compound verbs," "verb-adverb combinations," and so forth. We are dealing, of course, with structures like **put** *it* **on, call up** *Mr. Smith*, **take** *this information* **down,** in which a verb and a function word (adverb) work closely together to express a meaning. In addition, when an object is present, these words *may* be separated by noun objects and *must* be separated by unstressed pronoun objects. Such combinations are usually called "separable" two-word verbs.

We also have combinations like **get on** *the bus,* **look for** *the money,* **wait on** *the customers,* which are inseparable —we say **get on** *it,* **look for** *it,* **wait on** *them*—but which nevertheless are more intimately connected than a mere intransitive verb followed by a prepositional phrase.

In identifying the inseparable two-word verbs, we have relied almost entirely on meaning. There is some overlapping with *The Key to English Prepositions 2,* since that book treats combinations of verbs and prepositional phrases. Our criterion is this: if the meaning of a combination can be predicted on the basis of the meaning of the individual parts (*listen to, insist on*), it is called a verb followed by a preposition; if not (*look for, call on*), it is called a two-word verb.

Some students may need to use a bilingual dictionary along with this book, as the vocabulary has not been restricted. The Glossary at the end of the book lists about 400 combinations, with definitions. It is indicative of the productivity of the two-word verb in English that only 120 full verbs occur in the list; differences in meaning are

v

expressed by changing the function word. The Glossary is not exhaustive; new combinations are readily coined, and new meanings of existing combinations are constantly being created. Nevertheless the Glossary contains most of the meanings of most of the combination that the student is likely to encounter in reading and in informal conversation, and if he masters all those presented in this book he should have little difficulty in the future with two-word verbs.

It was intended that the material in the book be studied in sequence, since each lesson is based to a degree on preceding material. Nevertheless, individual exercises can be used at any time to teach a point if desired.

The dots used to indicate stress are adapted from those originated by Kenneth Croft and are used with his authorization and approval.

This book is one of the KEY TO ENGLISH series, prepared for the Collier Macmillan English Program by the Materials Development Staff of English Language Services, Inc., under the co-direction of Edwin T. Cornelius, Jr., and Willard D. Sheeler. *The Key to English Two-Word Verbs* was written by Earle W. Brockman and Winifred Jones.

CONTENTS

CONTENTS

INTRODUCTION

To the learner of English, one of the most irritating and frustrating aspects of the language is the formation of special expressions or idioms. The student discovers, to his dismay, that there are dozens of word combinations whose meaning bears little or no relationship to the individual words of which they are composed. He learns, for example, the words *call* and *off*, and then some time later discovers that there is a special expression *call off* which means "cancel." On another occasion he may encounter the expression *off and on* and be astonished to learn that this phrase is an expression of time, not one of place or location or direction. (It means "intermittently.")

And so it continues, a seemingly endless list of formations involving nouns, verbs, adjectives, adverbs, and function words without any apparent regard for logic in either construction or meaning. This process of combining individual words into new units having variant meanings is not peculiar to English, of course; similar idiomatic formations exist in all languages. Many such special expressions, in English as well as in other languages, are unpredictable and patternless because they are derived from cultural factors other than language, from folklore, from famous proverbs, even from politics and current events. Expressions such as "sitting duck" (*an easy target*), "pull someone's leg" (*tease* or *fool someone*), or "New Deal" (a particular governmental policy developed in the United States under President Franklin D. Roosevelt) have similarly picturesque counterparts in other languages. Phrases such as these are probably best learned one by one as separate vocabulary items.

In one area of this maze of special expressions, however, a more systematic approach is possible. The **two-word verb** occurs in sufficient numbers and with sufficient consistency in structural patterns to permit the formation of organized lists and certain rules of word order. Gram-

1

marians are not in complete agreement upon the definition of two-word verbs in English, nor, for that matter, even upon the existence of such a category. Many call them verb-adverb or verb-preposition combinations. But for the student of English the presentation of such groups of verbs along with certain guides to problems of word order, stress, and intonation is a definite aid in his study of the language. And this, of course, is the intent of this text-book: to provide a practice and guide book in the use of two-word verbs.

Definition of the Two-Word Verb

For the purpose of this text, we will say that the two-word verb in English has the following characteristics:

(a) The two-word verb consists of a verb followed by a function word that may also function in English sentences as a preposition.

(b) The two-word verb is a semantic unit having a meaning which often differs from the sum of the meanings of its individual parts.

(c) The two-word verb is a grammatical unit which fulfills normal verb functions in English sentences. It may or may not be followed by a noun object. Whether a following noun is the object of the verb or the object of the preposition following the verb is of little consequence here. We will call all such nouns simply "objects."

This is not presented as a definitive statement. Indeed, as we progress in our study of this particular problem in English grammar, we become more and more aware of the difficulties of making a complete classification of two-word verbs, and we will be forced to modify our definition at certain points.

Note on Stress and Intonation

Stress is the degree of loudness with which a syllable is spoken. English has three levels: loud, which will be represented in this book by a large dot ●; medium, represented by ●; and weak, represented by ·.

In addition, we must discuss **word stress.** Every word, as well as many compounds that are written as more than one word (for example, *look over*), has its own stress pattern. There is one loud stress, and the other syllables, if any, have medium or weak stress.

Examples:

<blockquote>

· ● ·   · ● ·
extinguish   look over
</blockquote>

There can be only one loud stress in each phrase. Therefore, when words are combined in phrases, the word stresses of all but one of them are reduced to medium or weak.

Examples:

<blockquote>

●   · · ● ·
out   out the window
</blockquote>

<blockquote>

●   · ●
put   put out
</blockquote>

<blockquote>

· · · ● ·
put it out the window
</blockquote>

It is always the word stress that is reduced. The other syllables of the word or phrase remain unchanged.

Intonation is the rise and fall of the pitch of the voice as one talks. It is closely bound up with stress, so much so that authorities disagree as to the best way to analyze these features and some of them insist that they cannot be treated separately. A detailed treatment of intonation is beyond the scope of this book. In general, if the intonation requires the pitch level of a phrase to change, it will change on the syllable that has loud stress. In a falling intonation pattern, as at the end of most statements, the pitch drops during the utterance of the loud syllable if it is the last one in the phrase and immediately after it if there are other syllables in the phrase.

This is not a complete statement of intonation phenomena, of course. There are many complications, and mastery of stress and intonation can come only after long practice and careful imitation of a good speaker of English.

Say these words and phrases:

●
put

●
look

● ●
put on

● ●
look out

● ● · ● · · ●
Put on your rubbers today.

● ● · · ●
Look out for the cars.

Review of Verbs and Prepositions

In our study of the two-word verb in English, let us first consider the form of this type of word grouping. According to our definition, a two-word verb consists of a verb followed by a second word which normally functions as a preposition. Since verbs and prepositions are integral parts of two-word verbs, we should first of all establish our definitions of these two types of words. Briefly, in review, a verb is any word which can have the endings -(e)s, -ing, and -(e)d (or certain irregular inflections) and which can appear in one or more of the following positions in English sentences:

Don't _____. (*go, laugh, smoke, worry*)
Don't _____ it. (*take, move, believe, repeat*)
They (You, We) _____ strange. (*are, seem, look, sound*)

A preposition is a function word that appears before nouns and relates the noun to some other construction in the sentence.

We walked _____ the park. (*in, through, around, toward*)
_____ our vacation we went to New York. (*During, Before, After*)
The package is _____ my new desk. (*in, on, under, near, by*)

Sentences for Practice

A. Practice these sentences, giving loud stress to the last word.

1. Don't play in the street.
2. Don't fall down the stairs.
3. Don't walk on the grass.

4. Don't speak to the guards.
5. Don't climb up the tree.
6. Don't run through the park.
7. Don't talk to the boys.
8. Don't stand by the door.
9. Don't drive near the lake.
10. Don't run down the hill.

B. Practice these sentences, each of which ends with a prepositional phrase.

1. We drove our car *around the block*.
2. She served ice cream *after dinner*.
3. I took a walk *along the river*.
4. She swept the dust *under the rug*.
5. They hung the painting *above the fireplace*.
6. He studies French *during the summer*.
7. I received a card *from my friends*.
8. We sent a notice *about the meeting*.
9. He threw a stone *across the lake*.
10. I explained the problem *to the class*.

C. Practice these sentences, each of which contains a noun followed by a prepositional phrase.

1. The boy *in the blue suit* is my brother.
2. The man *with the red hair* seems familiar.
3. The gift *for his wife* was beautiful.
4. The shop *across the street* looks familiar.
5. The apples *from this tree* taste delicious.
6. The roses *behind the house* smell fragrant.
7. The lock *on the door* feels loose.
8. The news *about the crisis* appears encouraging.
9. The train *to the city* was crowded.
10. The story *of his life* sounds interesting.

Exercises

A. Read the following paragraph. List all the verbs (including ing-forms and past participles). Then list all the prepositions (omitting *to* before verbs).

The children, of course, were delighted by the trip to the circus, and even the adults had to admit that they were pleased with the evening's performance. It was difficult to see everything, for the spectators had to choose among the spectacles in each of the three rings. The animal trainer, with his lions and tigers, was the first to appear in the center ring, while on the left, the high-wire artist performed under a glowing spotlight, and to the right a troupe of weight-lifters astonished the audience. The tricks of the trained dogs, jumping and dancing around the ring with their tiny red hats on their heads, especially pleased the children. The trapeze artists, swinging high above the crowd, were a thrilling sight of skill and grace. All in all, it was a lot of fun for everyone who went.

B. In each of the following sentences, substitute two or more different prepositions for those in italics. In the first, for example, the prepositions *before*, *after*, and *at* could be substituted for *until*, and the meaning of the sentence altered.

1. The bus won't leave *until* ten o'clock.
2. The children ran *to* the playground.
3. In the classroom, John sits *behind* Charles.
4. The post office is *near* the bank.
5. The Smiths live in the apartment *above* ours.
6. We will be in New York *in* three hours.
7. I met Mr. and Mrs. Carter *during* the dance.
8. Does this bus go *toward* the museum?

C. In each of the following sentences, substitute two or more different verbs for each verb in italics. For example, in the first, the verbs *fly*, *go*, and *travel* could be used instead of *drive*.

1. Next year we are going to *drive* to New York.
2. Have you *finished* all the lessons in the book?
3. The Andersons *painted* their house last week.
4. The guests are *waiting* in the living room.
5. My sister doesn't *want* to travel around the world.
6. When will they *report* the news to the public?
7. In the evening, I enjoy *talking* to my friends.
8. Do you intend to *work* in Philadelphia?

Examples of Two-Word Verbs

From the information presented in Lesson 1, we might expect that two-word verbs could be freely formed by combining the verbs presented in the first group of examples and the prepositions presented in the second group.

Verbs	Prepositions
go	in
laugh	through
smoke	around
worry	toward
take	during
move	before
believe	after
repeat	in
are	on
seem	under
look	near
sound	by

But such is not the case. We cannot "create" a two-word verb by arbitrarily combining any verb whatever with any preposition whatever. The problem of the student is not to make two-word verbs, but to recognize them.

Now we must differentiate between two-word verbs and normal verb-preposition sequences.

At this point let us refer to another section of our definition: a two-word verb is a semantic unit having a meaning which often differs from the sum of the meanings of its separate parts. Notice, for example, the contrasts in meaning in these two sentences using the sequence *call up*.

Please *call up* the stairs and wake the children.

(*Call* and *up* have their ordinary meanings.)

9

I want to *call up* the department store, but I don't know the number.

(*Call up* means "telephone.")

In the first sentence we have used *call* as a verb and *up* in a prepositional phrase, indicating direction. In the second sentence, however, *call up* has a meaning of its own: "telephone." *Call up*, then, is a typical two-word verb. Other examples are illustrated in the sentences below.

Verb + Prepositional Phrase	*Two-Word Verb*
The boys **ran** *into the street*.	Mr. Brown **ran into** an old friend yesterday. (*met by accident*)
The two housewives enjoy **talking** *over the fence*.	The committee is **talking over** our report. (*discussing*)
We **looked** *up the street* but saw no one.	Sally **looked up** the word because she didn't understand it. (*sought in a reference book*)
After **turning** *on Tenth Street,* drive north.	Don't you remember **turning on** the light? (*starting the operation of*)
Turn *off the highway* at the next intersection.	**Turn off** the radio, please. (*stop the operation of*)
I **waited** *on the corner* for an hour.	She **waited on** us quietly and efficiently. (*served*)
If you **look** *over the mountains,* you will see a rainbow.	The teacher will **look over** our tests tomorrow. (*examine*)
The passers-by **looked** *into the window* curiously.	Have the policemen **looked into** the bank robbery? (*investigated*)

These pairs of sentences illustrate differences not only in meaning, but also in the interior relationships of the sentence parts. The first column of sentences clearly illustrates the use of prepositional phrases as adverbial modifiers. For each of these sentences we can compose a question with "where" and give a meaningful answer by using the prepositional phrase.

Where did the boys run?	Into the street.
Where did the housewives talk?	Over the fence.
Where did we look?	Up the street.

If we form a question with "where" for the sentences in the second column, however, we find that there is no meaningful response.

Where did Mr. Brown run?	Into an old friend. (*not meaningful*)
Where is the committee talking?	Over the report. (*not meaningful*)

But when we formulate a question with "what" or "whom," using our two-word verb as *a unit,* we find that the meaning is clear.

Whom did Mr. Brown run into?	An old friend.
What is the committee looking over?	The report.
What did Sally look up?	The word.

We have now applied the last part of our definition: a two-word verb is a grammatical unit which fulfills the normal functions of a verb in a sentence. In all of the sentences above, we will consider the noun phrases which follow the two-word verbs as the objects of the two-word verbs, not as the objects of the prepositions. In other words, these two-word verbs have objects just like ordinary transitive verbs. Here are some other common two-word verbs that can have objects, with some of their meanings. (Many two-word verbs have several meanings, as the student will learn upon consulting the Glossary at the end of this book.)

bring about	*cause to happen*
bring up	*raise, care for from childhood*
call off	*cancel*
call on	*visit*
carry on	*continue*
carry out	*fulfill; complete*
come across	*discover accidentally*
get off	*descend from, leave* (e.g., *a public vehicle or other conveyance*)
get on	*mount, enter* (*a public vehicle, a horse*, etc.)
leave out	*omit*
look over	*examine*
make up	*invent, compose*
pick out	*select*
put off	*postpone*
put on	*dress in*
put out	*extinguish*
take up	*begin to study; prepare for a career in*

Sentences for Practice

A. Practice saying the following sentences aloud, paying particular attention to the differences in stress and the location of the pause. These differences occur primarily in slow, deliberate speech. In rapid speech, the differences tend to disappear.

1. I *called* | up the *stairs*.   I called *up* | my *niece*.
2. She *ran* | into the room.   She ran *into* | her *friend*.
3. We *looked* | up the street.   We looked *up* | the *words*.
4. They *turned* | on the highway.   They turned *on* | the *street lights*.
5. We *turned* | off the road.   We'll turn *off* | the *lamp*.
6. She *waited* | on the porch.   She's waiting *on* | the *guests*.

7. He *looked* | over the   He looked *over* | the *plans.*
   wall.
8. They *looked* | into the   They looked *into* | the
   box.   theft.

B. Practice these questions and answers.

1. What did they call off? The concert.
   They called off the concert.
2. Whom did you call on? My relatives.
   I called on my relatives.
3. What did she put out? The fire.
   She put out the fire.
4. What did they put off? The party.
   They put off the party.
5. What did he put on? His hat.
   He put on his hat.
6. What did they look over? The schedule.
   They looked over the schedule.
7. What did he look into? The problem.
   He looked into the problem.
8. What did you look up? His address.
   I looked up his address.

C. Practice these questions and answers.

1. Did Mr. Dawson select a gift?
   Yes, he picked out a nice gift.
2. Did the students omit a question?
   Yes, they left out question 10.
3. Did the Bradfords raise any children?
   Yes, they brought up both their nephew and their
   niece.
4. Did you discover any antiques?
   Yes, I came across a rare old clock.
5. Did the thief invent an alibi?
   Yes, he made up an unusual one.

6. .Did Joe begin to study engineering?
    Yes, he took up civil engineering.
7. Did the election cause any reforms?
    Yes, it brought about some political reforms.
8. Did the secretary complete her tasks?
    Yes, she carried out her duties.
9. Did the entertainers continue the show?
    Yes, they carried on the entertainment.

Exercises

A. Change the following sentences, using the correct form
of the two-word verb given at the left of each sentence in
place of the italicized verb.

Example: *call on*   I *visited* all my cousins last year.

                       *I called on all my cousins last
                       year*.

1. *put out*   The rain *extinguished* the huge forest
                 fire.
2. *make up*   John *invented* that joke about the talk-
                 ing dog.
3. *get off*   You should *leave* the bus at the corner
                 of First and Maple.
4. *look into*   We are going to *investigate* the dis-
                 appearance of the money.
5. *talk over*   The entire committee will *discuss* the
                 proposals.
6. *carry out*   The Parliament *fulfilled* the Prime Min-
                 ister's program.
7. *put off*   We'll have to *postpone* the dance until
                 next Friday.
8. *come across* Margaret *discovered* that quotation in
                 a poem.
9. *pick out*   Boys usually enjoy *selecting* gifts for
                 others.

10.	*bring about*	The chairman's orders *caused* a change in policy.
11.	*call up*	Bill often *telephones* his brother.
12.	*turn off*	They *extinguish* the street lights at the same time every morning.
13.	*wait on*	Ten young ladies *served* the customers.
14.	*call off*	The county fair was *canceled* because of financial difficulties.
15.	*run into*	Anne *met* a former high school classmate last week.
16.	*put on*	We have to *dress in* our best clothes for the dinner.
17.	*look over*	The Board of Education usually *examines* the class schedule.
18.	*leave out*	Please *omit* the last ten names on the list.
19.	*bring up*	The nurses *raised* the problem of overcrowding in the hospital.

B. Complete the following sentences by providing the proper function word to complete the two-word verb. The meaning of the two-word verb is given at the left of each sentence.

1.	*telephone*	When are you going to call _____ the Employment Office?
2.	*visit*	We often call _____ our next-door neighbors.
3.	*cancel*	Why was the conference called _____?
4.	*seek in a reference book*	I had to look _____ that address in the phone book.
5.	*examine*	The professor is looking _____ the homework.
6.	*investigate*	Will the supervisor look _____ the complaints?

7. *enter*   Where do we get _____ the bus for the station?

8. *leave*   We'll get _____ the train at the up-town station.

9. *raise*   Who brought _____ that problem at the meeting?

10. *cause*   The flood was brought _____ by several days of heavy rain.

11. *extinguish*   Please put _____ the lights before you leave.

12. *clothe oneself in*   The children had better put _____ their boots and raincoats.

13. *postpone*   I'm afraid they're going to have to put _____ the picnic.

14. *complete*   Have the laboratory technicians carried _____ the experiments?

15. *continue*   In spite of their bad luck, they decided to carry _____ their work.

C. Complete the answers to the questions below by using the appropriate form of one of the two-word verbs in the list.

come across	take up
leave out	talk over
make up	turn off
pick out	turn on
run into	wait on

1. Did you happen to see Helen last week?
   Yes, I _____ her when I was shopping.

2. Has Robert decided what he's going to study?
   Yes, he's going to _____ dentistry.

3. When are they going to discuss the plans for next year?
   They're going to _____ the plans sometime this month.

4. Why won't the car start?
   Well, you haven't _____ the motor yet!

5. Do you extinguish all the lights in the room when you watch TV?
   No, they say it's bad for the eyes to _____ all the lights.

6. Do most children enjoy inventing imaginary play-mates?
   Not all children _____ imaginary stories, but many do.

7. Who is the waitress serving the Smiths?
   Oh, that's Alice Woodson who is _____ Mr. and Mrs. Smith.

8. Where did you find that lovely painting?
   I _____ that picture in a little shop on Tenth Street.

9. Who selected the furniture for the apartment?
   I think Mrs. Gibson _____ all the furnishings.

10. Why did you omit the pepper from the recipe?
    I _____ the pepper because the meat is already well spiced.

D. Write complete answers to the following questions, using the same two-word verb that appears in the question.

1. Whom did the servants wait on?
2. What are the teachers talking over?
3. Whom did the Youngs bring up?
4. What did the cook leave out?
5. Whom do we have to call on?
6. What are the children picking out?
7. What must the students look up?
8. Whom did you run into downtown?
9. What did she say to turn off?
10. What are you going to put on for the party?

LESSON 3

The Two Types of Two-Word Verbs with Noun Objects

Two-word verbs, as we have stated, function as single units in both meaning and construction. We have seen that some two-word verbs can have objects, just like ordinary verbs.

We **looked up** *the words.*	We **found** *the words.*
I didn't **leave out** *any questions.*	I didn't **omit** *any questions.*
Have you **called on** *Mrs. Price?*	Have you **visited** *Mrs. Price?*

So far, then, the problem of two-word verbs seems to be one of meaning only. The verbs function with normal inflections and with the ordinary auxiliary verbs in statements and questions. Their word order looks perfectly normal. Unfortunately, things are not quite that simple. There is a rather large set of two-word verbs called *separable.* These verbs are peculiar in that they *allow* their two parts to be separated by short noun objects and *require* that they be so separated when the direct object is an unstressed personal pronoun (*me, you, him, her, it, us, them*). In other words, the noun object of a separable two-word verb may come between the two parts, or it may follow them both; a pronoun object *must* come between them. Of the verbs used as examples above, *look up* and *leave out* are separable; *call on* is not.

We *looked up* the words.	We *looked* them *up.*
I *left out* some questions.	I *left* them *out.*

The student must learn in each case whether a two-word verb is separable or not. While great efforts have been made by grammarians to classify these expressions according to logical or formal criteria, not much has been learned

18

that is of use to the student of English. It is only practice and habit, in the long run, that will tell him which is which.

Here are some more examples of separable two-word verbs, this time with noun objects in both positions:

> I *picked out* the tie myself.
> I *picked* the tie *out* myself.
>
> They've *called off* the game.
> They've *called* the game *off*.
>
> I *called up* Mary.
> I *called* Mary *up*.

Many other two-word verbs that are followed by objects are never separated, whether the object is a noun or a pronoun.

Did you see Mrs. Lake?	Yes, I *ran into* her yesterday.
Where do I take the bus?	You can *get on* it at the corner.
Have they investigated the matter?	Yes, they're *looking into* it now.

In order to distinguish between these two kinds of verbs, we will label all two-word verbs as **separable** or **inseparable.** The verbs already mentioned in this book are classified as follows:

Separable		Inseparable
bring about	make up	call on
bring up	pick out	come across
call off	put off	get off
call up	put on	get on
carry on	put out	look into
carry out	take up	run into
leave out	talk over	wait on
look over	turn off	
look up	turn on	

Listed below are further two-word verbs in common use, with definitions, classified according to whether they are separable or inseparable.

Two-Word Verbs That Are Separable When Followed by an Object

blow up	*cause to explode*
burn down	*destroy by burning*
cross out	*eliminate*
do over	*redo*
figure out	*interpret, understand*
fill out	*complete (a printed form)*
find out	*discover*
have on	*be dressed in*
hold off	*delay*
make over	*remake*
pick up	*take or lift with the hands or fingers*
point out	*indicate*
put away	*store; put in the proper place*
take off	*remove*
think over	*consider*
throw away	*discard*
try on	*put on (a garment) to verify the fit*
try out	*test, use experimentally*
wear out	*use (something) until it is no longer usable*

Two-Word Verbs That Are Inseparable When Followed by an Object

care for	*like; guard, supervise, maintain, tend*
get in	*enter (a vehicle, enclosed space)*
get over	*recover from*
get through	*finish*
go over	*review*
go with	*harmonize with, be compatible with*
hear from	*receive a communication from*
look for	*seek*
see about.	*consider, arrange*
take after	*resemble*

Sentences for Practice

A. Practice the following sentences, placing the loud stress on the last word.

1. He called his sister up.	He called her up.
2. We called the meeting off.	We called it off.
3. She looked the answer up.	She looked it up.
4. They turned the engine on.	They turned it on.
5. I picked the present out.	I picked it out.
6. We put the fires out.	We put them out.
7. We brought the children up.	We brought them up.
8. I took the subject up.	I took it up.
9. They put the jackets on.	They put them on.
10. She turned the drier off.	She turned it off.
11. We left the answer out.	We left it out.
12. They put the picnic off.	They put it off.
13. He made the story up.	He made it up.
14. I took the hat off.	I took it off.

B. Practice the following pairs of sentences. Place the loud stress on the last word, or the usually stressed syllable of the last word.

1. We talked over the problem.
   We talked it over.
2. I looked over the homework.
   I looked it over.
3. He brought about these changes.
   He brought them about.
4. She carried out her plans.
   She carried them out.
5. Will picked up the wallet.
   Will picked it up.

6. Bess wore out her shoes.
   Bess wore them out.
7. Bob tried on the coat.
   Bob tried it on.
8. We found out the answer.
   We found it out.
9. They put away the blankets.
   They put them away.
10. Paul pointed out the museum.
    Paul pointed it out.
11. She threw away the rags.
    She threw them away.
12. They blew up the bridge.
    They blew it up.
13. They burned down the barn.
    They burned it down.
14. I made over my blouse.
    I made it over.

C. In the first of each pair of sentences, stress the direct object. In the second sentence of the pair, stress the function word.

1. We looked into the problem. We looked into it.
2. She ran into a friend. She ran into her.
3. They got on the train. They got on it.
4. We got off the bus. We got off it.
5. He got over his cold. He got over it.
6. They went over the lessons. They went over them.
7. He takes after his father. He takes after him.
8. I got through the test. I got through it.
9. He got in the car. He got in it.
10. They saw through the trick. They saw through it.

D. Practice these sentences, putting the stress on the last word of the first sentence. In the second sentence, put the stress on the verb.

● ● · ● · ●
1. I waited on the guests.
2. He called on his neighbor.
3. I heard from my brother.
4. She looked for her glasses.

· ● · ·
I waited on them.
He called on him.
I heard from him.
She looked for them.

Exercises

A. Complete the answer to each question by filling in the blank with the correct form of a two-word verb from the list.

blow up	make over
call up	point out
cross out	put out
do over	take off
figure out	talk over
find out	think over
hold off	throw away
look over	

1. Why are they delaying their decision for so long?
   They're _____ it _____ because of changing conditions.

2. Can you remake this dress?
   Yes, I think I can _____ it _____.

3. Did anyone discover what their new address is?
   No, we couldn't _____ it _____.

4. Didn't anyone indicate the museums to you?
   Yes, the guide _____ them _____ to us.

5. Should a man remove his hat indoors?
   Yes, he should _____ it _____ when he is inside.

6. Won't you please consider my proposals?
   Well, I'll _____ them _____ and let you know.

7. Can the professor read the inscription?
   No, he can't _____ it _____.

8. Does the school discard all of its waste paper?
   Yes, they _____ it _____ once a week.

9. When should we telephone for a cab?
   _____ them _____ when we're ready to leave the house.

10. How was the bridge destroyed?
    The enemy _____ it _____ with explosive..

11. How can you extinguish a small grease fire in a pan?
    You can _____ it _____ with a handful of baking soda.

12. Do I have to redo my homework?
    Yes, you must _____ it _____ unless you want to fail.

13. Did Mr. and Mrs. Fuller examine the new house?
    I'm sure they _____ it _____ very carefully.

14. Why did they eliminate the word "very"?
    They _____ it _____ because they thought it was unnecessary.

15. Let's discuss the question privately.
    All right, we'll _____ it _____ at my house.

B. Rewrite each sentence with the direct object between the two parts of the verb unit. Then write the sentence with a pronoun object.

> Example: He reached down and picked up the newspaper.
>
> > *He reached down and picked the newspaper up.*
> >
> > *He reached down and picked it up.*

1. The raging fire burned down the old wooden building.

2. Constant use will wear out any machine.

3. I'd like to try on that blue wool coat.
4. You ought to try out that radio before you buy it.
5. Mrs. Lowell had on her new dress last night.
6. The applicants have to fill out several forms.
7. The workmen put away their tools and left the factory.
8. Did the firemen put out the fire?
9. Who threw away these perfectly good books?
10. Don't take off your coat; it's cold in here.
11. Arnold can't figure out his algebra problems.
12. You'll have to cross out the mistakes.
13. Why is Mr. Watson holding off his decision?
14. Please do over yesterday's assignment.

C. Answer these questions using a personal pronoun as the direct object form.

> Examples: Have you heard from your brother William?
> *No, I haven't heard from him.*
> Did Arthur get over the shock of his father's death?
> *Yes, he got over it.*

1. Will this blue sofa go with the green carpet? No,
   _____.
2. Did the class go over the words? Yes, _____.
3. Isn't Mr. Thompson going to see about the reservations for the concert? Yes, _____.
4. Does your daughter take after you? No, _____.
5. Don't you care for this kind of candy? No, _____.
6. Did the policeman see through the thief's story? Yes,
   _____.
7. Has Mr. Porter looked for his lost watch at his office? Yes, _____.

8. Did you come across this theory in your research?
   Yes, _____.

9. Is Miss Glover going to call on the Nelsons? Yes,
   _____.

10. Have the union members looked into the proposed
    contract? No, _____.

D. Complete the following sentences by using one of the following two-word verbs: get on, get off, get over, get through, get in. The meanings to be expressed are given to the left of each sentence.

1.	*enter*	In English, we say that we _____ a bus or train, but we _____ a car or a taxi.
2.	*recover from*	It isn't easy to _____ a serious illness.
3.	*finish*	The construction crew must _____ with the job before winter begins.
4.	*leave*	Be sure to _____ the bus before it turns the corner.
5.	*enter*	Passengers are not supposed to _____ a bus through the back door.
6.	*recover from*	The ABC Company has never really _____ the losses from the fire two years ago.
7.	*enter*	I always lock the car door after I _____.
8.	*finish*	Do the farmers expect to _____ with the plowing this week?
9.	*leave*	Mr. Salter _____ the bus too soon, and lost his way.
10.	*finish*	Hurry up! We have to _____ all these papers before five o'clock.

E. Answer the following questions, using the pronoun *it*, *him*, *her*, or *them* in your answer.

> Examples: Did you look up the word?
> *Yes, I looked it up.*
>
> Is she looking for her gloves?
> *Yes, she's looking for them.*

1. Will they look into the problem? Yes, _____.
2. Has he looked over the plan? Yes, _____.
3. Should I put on my hat? Yes, _____.
4. Has he put off the lecture? Yes, _____.
5. Can they put out the fire? Yes, _____.
6. Did you put away your typewriter? Yes, _____.
7. Should he try out the pen? Yes, _____.
8. Is she going to call up her cousin Mary? Yes, _____.
9. Did she pick up the broken glasses? Yes, _____.
10. Did you pick out that chair? Yes, _____.
11. Will you turn on the TV? Yes, _____.
12. Can you turn off the machine? Yes, _____.
13. Did she take up nursing? Yes, _____.
14. Should they take off their coats? Yes, _____.
15. Does he take after his father? Yes, _____.

LESSON 4

Inseparable Two-Word Verbs

Most of the two-word verbs presented in the previous lessons are classified as **separable.** It is easy to recognize a separable two-word verb: any combination of verb and function word that can be separated by a noun object is a separable two-word verb. When we come to **inseparable** combinations of verbs and function words, however, it is not quite so easy to identify the two-word verbs. In fact, many analysts do not recognize the existence of the inseparable two-word verb; they treat all such combinations as verb + adverb if no noun follows, or verb + prepositional phrase if a noun follows. This is sound grammar, but the fact remains that *in meaning* a great many combinations function as though they were single units. In other words, they comply with the third part of our definition of the two-word verb, especially when the meaning of the combination is not easily predicted from the meanings of its individual parts.

In many cases the student's problem is not that of learning a phrase with a new meaning, but of associating a verb with the proper preposition: *listen to, look at, insist (up) on, wait for.* This type of inseparable combination is treated in *The Key to English Prepositions 2.*

Following are some examples of inseparable combinations that we will treat here as two-word verbs, largely because their meaning is not easily understood on the basis of the meanings of their parts:

bear on	*be related to, have to do with*
break in(to)	*interrupt (a conversation)*
call for	*come to get; require*
call on	*pay a formal visit to; invite to speak in a public meeting*

count on	*rely on*
disagree with	*cause illness or discomfort to* (usually said of food or drink; a facetious use of its literal meaning)
do without	*abstain from (something* needed or desirable*)*
figure on	*estimate; expect*
get around	*evade, avoid*
go with	*look pleasing together* (of colors, furniture, clothing, etc.); *accompany a person of the opposite sex in public, for courtship*
go without	*abstain from (something* needed or desirable*)*
hang around	*remain idly in the vicinity of*
hear of	*learn about*
hit on	*discover accidentally*
keep to	*persist, continue*
live on	*sustain or support oneself by means of*
look after	*take care of*
pick on	*tease, bully, tyrannize,* usually in petty but humiliating ways
run across	*find or meet accidentally*
run against	*compete against (in an election)*
run for	*be a candidate for (an elective office)*
run over	*hit with a car or other vehicle*
see to	*arrange, supervise, take responsibility for*
settle on	*decide on, choose, after a period of uncertainty*
stand for	*represent; permit, endure; be a candidate for (an elective office* in Great Britain)
stick to	*persist, persevere*
tell on	*report (a child's) misbehavior to someone in authority*
touch on	*mention briefly in speech or writing*

Dialog

A: Why does Al Baxter hang around the athletic field so much?

B: He likes sports, I guess. I often run across him at the bowling alley, too.

A: Doesn't he have a job? What does he live on?

B: Oh, sure, he works. He doesn't have to go without money. He's on the night shift at the factory. He gets pretty good wages.

A: Well, he certainly keeps at his sports! Doesn't he have any other interests?

B: Yeah, girls! He's going with Barbara Weller now. I see him calling for her every evening.

A: I never heard of her. Is she from this part of town?

B: She just moved here last month. She looks after the Drews' children during the day.

A: Oh, yes, I've seen her. I wish she would make the older Drew boy stop picking on the younger children at the playground. He breaks into their games and causes a lot of unpleasantness.

B: He should learn to stick to his own affairs. But he's only a child still. He will learn good behavior as he gets older.

Sentences for Practice

1. What does a bear live on?   It lives on fruit and fish.

2. What can you do without?   I can do without cigarettes.

3. Whom did Arthur run across?   He ran across Walter.

4. Which dress did she settle on?   She settled on the green dress.

5. Whom will he run against?	He'll run against Joe Wilkins.
6. What office are you running for?	I'm running for mayor.
7. Whom did they call for?	They called for their guests.
8. Whom can we count on?	We can count on Francis.
9. Whom is Bob going with?	He's going with Lillian.
10. Whom did the boys pick on?	They picked on the girls.
11. Whom did she look after?	She looked after the children.
12. Whom did he tell on?	He told on his brother.
13. What must we do without?	We must do without sugar.
14. What subject did he touch on?	He touched on theoretical physics.

Exercises

A. Complete the following sentences by choosing one of the two-word verbs in the list. Meanings are given at the left of each sentence.

bear on	live on
call on	pick on
count on	settle on
figure on	tell on
hit on	touch on

1. *sustain oneself*   Can you manage to _____ twenty-five dollars a week?

2. *mention*   The TV program will _____ the problem of public health.

3. *tease*   Why are the boys _____ the smaller
                  children?

4. *ask to*   The chairman will _____ Mr. Hunt to
   speak   give a report.

5. *report the*   Naughty little children often _____
   bad   each other.
   behavior of

6. *rely upon*   Donald is very busy; don't _____ him
                  for any help.

7. *estimate*   We'll have to _____ spending at least
                  five hundred dollars for the dance.

8. *discover*   Millie suddenly _____ an exciting idea.

9. *decide*   Can't the members of the committee
                  _____ the details later?

10. *relate to*   Does this book _____ the same subject
                  as the others in the series?

B. Complete the following sentences by using one of these
two-word verbs: *run into, run across, run over, run for, run
against.*

1. Do many people usually _____ the governorship?

2. Perhaps we'll _____ each other again sometime.

3. It was a terrible accident. A bus _____ several
   people.

4. Would you ever want to _____ a public office in
   your state?

5. We accidently _____ a rabbit with our car while
   we were out driving.

6. Where did you _____ that information?

7. Unexpectedly, she _____ her former teacher.

8. Hoover _____ Roosevelt for the Presidency of the
   United States in 1932.

9. We _____ some interesting paintings at the antique
   shop.

C. Answer each question below by filling in the blank with a two-word verb from the list.

bear on	get around
break into	go without
call for	live on
call on	see to
disagree with	stand for
figure on	stick to

1. Do all birds eat insects as their main food?
   No, some birds _____ seeds.
2. Do vegetables upset your stomach?
   Yes, all vegetables _____ me.
3. Have you ever tried eating only two meals a day?
   No, I've never _____ my third meal.
4. Doesn't Jack like to recite in class?
   No, he doesn't like to be _____.
5. Will the next chapter be related to political problems?
   Yes, the fifth chapter will _____ politics.
6. What do the stars in the U.S. flag represent?
   They _____ the fifty states.
7. Does that speaker always wander away from his topic?
   That's right. He doesn't usually _____ his subject.
8. How many pounds of fruit will the restaurant need?
   The chef always _____ at least fifty pounds.
9. Who is going to make the arrangements for the conference?
   The vice-president is going to _____ it.
10. Will Mr. and Mrs. Jackson come here and take us to the movie?
    Yes, they're going to _____ us at about eight o'clock.
11. How are the farmers going to avoid the flooding problem?
    We don't know how they're going to _____ it.
12. Is it polite to interrupt a conversation?
    You should never _____ anyone's conversation.

D. Complete the following sentences by choosing the correct word of the two given at the left of each sentence.

1. *of, from*   Haven't you ever heard _____ Shakespeare?

2. *on, out*   The accountants are trying to figure _____ these financial reports.

3. *through, to*   The nurses must see _____ the comfort of their patients.

4. *for, up*   Someone called me _____ late last night.

5. *around, over*   Mrs. Cline got _____ her sickness very quickly.

6. *out, on*   The architect has to pick _____ a new site for his building.

7. *over, across*   Be careful on the street so you don't get run _____.

8. *up, into*   When you're learning a new language, you often have to look _____ new words in your dictionary.

9. *at, for*   We'll wait _____ you in front of the library.

10. *for, against*   Who is going to run _____ Mr. Lyon in the election?

11. *up, about*   Robert and Paula were brought _____ by their grandparents.

12. *with, without*   It's dangerous for a person to go _____ water for a long time.

13. *over, for*   Janice lost her glasses and now she is looking _____ them.

14. *off, on*   Why did they call _____ the celebration?

15.	*over, through*	Can't we get _____ our work tonight?
16.	*off, on*	Put _____ your coat, please.
17.	*up, on*	Did anyone call _____ him?
18.	*up, off*	When did Ralph decide to take _____ medicine?
19.	*off, out*	Always put _____ your match before you drop it on the ground.
20.	*on, in*	Mr. Dodds got _____ his car and drove directly home.

E. Answer these questions, using the pronoun *it*.

1. Did you look up the word? Yes, _____.
2. Will she look over the report? Yes, _____.
3. Have the police looked into the murder? Yes, _____.
4. Is George looking for his book? Yes, _____.
5. Are you looking at this program? Yes, _____.
6. Will he look after the dog? Yes, _____.
7. Did he get on the bus? Yes, _____.
8. Will she get off the train? Yes, _____.
9. Did Tom get over his cold? Yes, _____.
10. Will we get through the work? Yes, _____.
11. Can they all get in that car? Yes, _____.
12. Did she get around the problem? Yes, _____.

LESSON 5

Two-Word Verbs Without Objects

So far, we have limited our discussion to two-word verbs that have noun objects. These we have divided into two groups: separable and inseparable. With two-word verbs that *do not* have objects, there is no problem of separability, for there is, of course, no direct object in the sentence structure.

It is not easy to distinguish two-word verbs without objects from the normal sequence of intransitive verb + adverb. However, the grammatical analysis is not a problem of very great importance to the learner of English. It *is* important, however, to learn the special meanings of the various combinations and to memorize the proper combinations of verbs and function words.

Some of the more common two-word verbs without objects are scarcely distinguishable from the verb-adverb sequence:

> You should *stand up* when an elderly person enters the room.
>
> The doctor told him to *lie down* for an hour.
>
> Please *step aside* and *turn around*.
>
> Why did the boy *run away*?
>
> What's *going on* here?

Others carry the meaning of the verb but not of the function word. That is, the function word seems to be rather unnecessary, so far as meaning is concerned.

> Why didn't you *wake up* this morning?
>
> *Move over* so the others can sit down.
>
> The children *ran off* to play in the park.
>
> The bus *slowed up* at the corner.

Still other two-word verbs have meanings that vary greatly from the individual meanings of their two separate parts.

> The meeting *turned out* to be interesting. (*proved*)
>
> I wish that man would *shut up!* (*stop talking;* an impolite, rather vulgar expression)
>
> How did the accident *come about?* (*happen*)
>
> You'll have to *back up* and turn around. (*go backwards*)

Other common two-word verbs without noun objects are these:

break down	*cease to function properly*
break out	*appear, arise suddenly or violently*
drop out (of)	*abandon some organized activity*
fall through	*fail; not be accomplished*
get up	*rise* (from bed, from a sitting or lying position)
give in	*surrender, stop resisting*
go off	*explode* (as fireworks)
go out	*stop burning* (said of a fire or a light)
hang up	*replace* (*a telephone receiver on its hook*)
let up	*diminish in intensity*
pass away	*die*
show up	*arrive, appear*
wear off	*fade, disappear*

Some of the verbs listed in this lesson may also occur with objects, with the same basic meaning. They are **separable** in this usage.

> Examples: *Turn* the car *around* and *back* it *up.*
>
> I have to *wake up* the children and *get* them *up* every morning.

hang up	shut up
move over	stand up
run off	slow up

Some of the verbs presented in earlier lessons with objects also occur without objects. In most cases, the meaning without an object is the same as the meaning with an object.

Separable verbs which can also occur without objects:

blow up	hold off
call up	turn up
find out	wear out

Inseparable verbs which can also occur without objects:

get in	get on
get off	get through

Sentences for Practice

A. Practice saying these sentences, putting the stress on the function word.

1. Stand up.   Please stand up.   Please don't stand up.
2. Get in.   Please get in.   Please don't get in.
3. Find out.   Please find out.   Please don't find out.
4. Get off.   Please get off.   Please don't get off.
5. Lie down.   Please lie down.   Please don't lie down.
6. Give in.   Please give in.   Please don't give in.
7. Back up.   Please back up.   Please don't back up.
8. Wake up.   Please wake up.   Please don't wake up.
9. Get up.   Please get up.   Please don't get up.

B. Practice saying these sentences. Stress the function word.

1. He got in.   He got in it.
2. He got off.   He got off it.
3. He got through.   He got through it.
4. He got on.   He got on it.

C. Practice saying these sentences. In each case the function word is stressed.

1. The lamp went out.
2. The gun went off.
3. The rain let up.
4. The students dropped out.
5. The family got up.
6. The fog wore off.
7. The plan fell through.
8. The car broke down.
9. The officers gave in.
10. The patient passed away.

D. Practice saying these sentences.

1. I woke up the children.
   I woke the children up.
   I woke them up.

2. They ran off the dogs.
   They ran the dogs off.
   They ran them off.

3. He slowed up the car.
   He slowed the car up.
   He slowed it up.

4. The children wore out the chairs.
   They wore the chairs out.
   They wore them out.

5. I hung up the phone.
   I hung the phone up.
   I hung it up.

6. I called up my mother.
   I called my mother up.
   I called her up.

7. They held off the enemy army.
   They held the enemy army off.
   They held it off.

8. We found out the secret.
   We found the secret out.
   We found it out.

Exercises

A. Change the italicized words or groups of words to a two-word verb.

1. Did the experiment *prove* to be successful?
2. Please don't *put the telephone on its hook.*
3. When did these events *happen?*
4. Most of the audience *appeared* late.
5. What made the dynamite *explode?*
6. The storm has *lessened* at last.
7. Her parents *relented* and let her buy a new dress.
8. Mrs. Emmons' father *died* last night.
9. The excitement of the children *faded* gradually.
10. Why did the experiment *fail?*

B. Write answers to these questions, using a two-word verb from the list.

back up	get up
break down	go out
break out	show up
come about	wear off

1. When did World War I begin?
2. Why didn't Mrs. Lane appear at the reception?
3. Why did the fire in the fireplace stop burning?
4. What time do the children usually rise?
5. Why is that car going backwards?
6. How quickly did the paint on the new toys come off?
7. How did the accident happen?
8. Why has that machine stopped operating?

C. Complete the following sentences with a two-word verb. The meaning is given at the left of each sentence.

1. *lessen* When is this hot weather going to _____?

2. *explode* Did the balloon _____?

3. *rise* We'll have to _____ early to catch the six o'clock train.

4. *break the connection* It really isn't polite to _____ when someone is speaking to you on the phone.

5. *telephone* Will your supervisor _____ before the meeting?

6. *raise* Mrs. Grant has _____ eleven children.

7. *lift* Please _____ the paper from the floor.

8. *appear* John didn't _____ at the conference.

9. *be found* I lost an earring last week, and today it _____ in the pocket of my dress.

10. *wake* Walter usually _____ at exactly six-thirty every morning.

11. *invent* Mr. Kent _____ an interesting story for the class to enact.

12. *seek in a reference book* Let's _____ this information in the encyclopedia.

13. *be quiet* Father shouted angrily at the children, "_____!"

14. *drive backwards* The driver was _____ when the accident happened.

15. *reduce the speed* I always _____ when I approach this corner.

D. Change the italicized objects of the two-word verbs to personal pronouns. Change the word order if the verb is separable.

> Examples: Elizabeth woke up *her sister* early in the morning.
>
> *Elizabeth woke her up early in the morning.*
>
> Walter got on *the train* at 11 o'clock.
> *Walter got on it at 11 o'clock.*

1. Please move over *your books* so I can write a letter.
2. He wore out *his new shoes* in less than a month.
3. Steven got off *the bus* before it stopped and nearly caused an accident.
4. Turn on *the TV*.
5. The ranchers ran off *the mountain lions*.
6. Did the public health officials find out *the answer*?
7. The students got through *their homework* very quickly.
8. The directors will hold off *their announcement* until next month.
9. I always get in *my car* on the right-hand side.
10. The engineers blew up *that hill* to make room for the roadway.

E. Complete these sentences using the correct function word.

1. You have to turn _____ the motor before the car will start.
2. That light is shining in my eyes. Please turn it _____.
3. I heard something behind me, so I turned _____ to see what it was.
4. That lost ring will turn _____ somewhere, I'm sure.
5. The experiments with that new fertilizer turned _____ very well.
6. This street is much too narrow to turn _____ in.

7. The electricity can be turned _____ only by the chief engineer.

8. How many people turned _____ for the meeting?

9. I don't know how the new courses are going to turn _____.

10. Please turn _____ the radio so that the other residents can sleep.

LESSON 6

"Families" of Two-Word Verbs

From the examples of two-word verbs already presented, it is clear that there are certain function words, such as *out, off, on, for, of,* etc., which appear in many two-word verb units, separable and inseparable, with and without objects. Usually, these function words do not have consistent meanings in the two-word verbs of which they are a part. There are, however, a few "families," so to speak, of two-word verbs in which the function word carries a fairly consistent meaning. The word *up,* for example, often has the meaning of "completely" or "thoroughly." The following combinations are separable forms:

Please *clean up* your room. I *cleaned* it *up* yesterday.
Did Mary *drink up* her milk? Yes, she *drank* it *up* without complaining.

Other verbs of this type are:

add up	fix up
burn up	light up
chew up	mix up
count up	tie up
dress up	wash up
eat up	write up
fill up	

Up also appears in some verb units with the meaning "into small pieces."

Why did she *tear* that letter *up?*
Let's *cut up* the wood so we can *burn* it *up.*
The butcher *chopped up* the meat for me.
Why did the children *break up* their play house?

44

The word *down* appears in a few separable verb units, carrying the meaning "completely" or "in a downward direction."

burn down	push down
chop down	take down
cut down	tear down (*destroy*)
pull down	

There is a small group of two-word verbs, mostly related in meaning to the verb *clean,* which uses the word *off* to refer to "the surface of," or the word *out* to refer to "the inside of." These units, like those listed above, are separable.

Please *wipe off* the table before dinner.
Did you *sweep out* the closet last week?
Once a week I *clean out* the desk and *dust* it *off*.

brush off	brush out
rinse off	rinse out
wash off	wash out
wipe off	wipe out
clear off	clean out
dust off	

The word *over* appears in combination with several verbs. It often implies a destination. When there is a noun object these two-word verbs are separable.

Without Objects

Won't you *come over* to our house tonight?
Let's *drop over* to the cafe for a little while.
When did Thomas *go over* there?
Shall we *walk over* or *ride over*?
Our guests *stayed over* until Tuesday.
John is *flying over* to England this summer.

Separable, With Objects

Can you *bring* your snapshots *over* with you?

When did Alice *take* the books *over* to the library?

Let's *invite* some people *over* next week.

The secretary will *send* the information *over* by messenger.

We'll have to *carry* our groceries *over* to the car.

Another common word in two-word verbs is *back*, which, with the verb, brings the meaning of "return." As with the *over* group, there may or may not be objects. Verbs with objects are separable.

Without Objects

When are the students *coming back?*

The tourists *went back* to Europe a week ago.

Will you *fly back* or *drive back?*

How long did it take the children to *walk back?*

Separable

The Donaldsons had to *take* their TV set *back* to the store.

We have to *pay* the money *back* in six weeks.

The boys forgot to *give* the ball *back.*

Are they going to *send* Frank *back* for another year of school?

Sentences for Practice

A. Practice saying these imperative sentences. In each sentence, place the loud stress on the last word in the sentence.

1. Clean up your room.

   Clean your room up.   Clean it up.

2. Eat up your food.

   Eat your food up.   Eat it up.

3. Fix up your clothes.
     Fix your clothes up.   Fix them up.
4. Fill up the bottle.
     Fill the bottle up.   Fill it up.
5. Tie up the package.
     Tie the package up.   Tie it up.
6. Burn up the trash.
     Burn the trash up.   Burn it up.
7. Drink up your milk.
     Drink your milk up.   Drink it up.
8. Cut up the wood.
     Cut the wood up.   Cut it up.
9. Count up the cash.
     Count the cash up.   Count it up.

B. Practice saying these questions and answers.

1. Did they chop the tree down?
     They chopped it down.
2. Did they burn the house down?
     They burned it down.
3. Did they take the pictures down?
     They took them down.
4. Did they pull the poles down?
     They pulled them down.
5. Did they tear the building down?
     They tore it down.
6. Did they push the door down?
     They pushed it down.

C. Practice saying these questions and answers.

1. Did you clean the car?
   Yes, I washed it off and cleaned it out.
2. Did you clean your desk?
   Yes, I dusted it off and cleared it out.

3. Did you clean the bookcase?
   Yes, I wiped it off and brushed it out.
4. Did you clean the teapot?
   Yes, I washed it off and rinsed it out.

Exercises

A. Make two new sentences like each of those listed below, by adding the word over and then the word back.

Example: Mr. and Mrs. Gates came at 8 o'clock.

> *Mr. and Mrs. Gates came over at 8 o'clock.*
>
> *Mr. and Mrs. Gates came back at 8 o'clock.*

1. The mechanic brought the car to us after fixing it.
2. Will the factory send the parts as soon as possible?
3. I want to take the photographs to the studio.
4. At 8 p.m., the speaker will go to the lecture hall.
5. Let's walk to the house.
6. The Bakers have invited us to a party next week.
7. The box is too heavy; the boys can't carry it for you.

B. Change the italicized objects in these sentences to *it* or *them* and put them in the correct position.

1. You'll have to chop up *this wood* before you burn it.
2. Aren't they going to light up *all the monuments* tonight?
3. It will be cheaper to tear down *that building* and build a new one rather than to fix up *such an old one*.
4. A small child has to learn to chew up *its food*.
5. Johnny has mixed up *the people in the story*.
6. The cashier is adding up *her receipts*.
7. Which reporter is going to write up *this news story*?
8. The fireman had to push down *the doors of the burning building*.
9. The builders are cutting down *the trees*.
10. Are you good at tying up *fancy packages*?

Other Constructions With Two-Word Verbs

A Two-Word Linking Verb

In our definition of the two-word verb, we stated that it is a grammatical unit which fulfills normal verb functions in English sentences. We have discovered that the two-word verb has the same forms as an ordinary verb, that it may occur in all kinds of sentences (questions, negative forms, etc.), and that it may or may not have a noun object. There is one kind of verb, however, that has very few examples among the two-word verbs, namely, linking verbs. A linking verb, you will remember, is one that can be followed by an adjective or a noun, with the following word either describing the subject or giving another name for the subject. (She *looks* beautiful. He *became* king.) There is only one linking verb of the two-word type: *turn into*, which is inseparable and means "become." It can be followed by noun complements but not by adjectives.

> In the fairy story, the frog *turned into* a prince.
> The friendly discussion had *turned into* a violent argument.

Adverbial Modifiers With Two-Word Verbs

The placement of adverbial modifiers in English sentences is a very complicated matter, and we do not intend to attempt to cover all of it here. In respect to two-word verbs, there is a difference in the behavior of the separable and inseparable ones with regard to adverbial modifiers.

You will remember that adverbs of manner (*slowly, carefully, politely*) regularly come just after the verb and before a prepositional phrase:

She came *slowly* into the room.

We walked *carefully* along the edge of the cliff.

She spoke *politely* to her guests.

This word order is allowed in the case of what we have called **inseparable** two-word verbs. In other words, the two-word verb is "inseparable" only in the sense that the function word is never separated from the verb by a direct object; it may be separated by an adverbial modifier, and in fact often is.

The children *laughed* heartily *at* the clown.

The audience *waited* eagerly *for* the beginning of the show.

Adverbial modifiers of **separable** two-word verbs, on the other hand, are never placed between the two parts. If, for instance, we wish to add the adverb *quickly* to the sentence "I found out the answer," we may say:

I found out the answer *quickly*.

or

I *quickly* found out the answer.

We may *not* say "I found quickly out the answer." This word order is not English.

Noun Objects Consisting of Several Words

We have seen that, in the case of separable two-word verbs, the noun object may come either between the two parts or after them both.

I *put* my hat *on*.

or: I *put on* my hat.

If the noun object is very long, however, English speakers avoid putting it between the two parts of the verb.

I put on *the hat I had bought the day before*.

Not: I put the hat I had bought the day before on.

It is difficult to make a rule on this, except that nouns with following modifiers are not ordinarily placed between the parts of the two-word verb. In case of doubt, the student should let the noun object follow the two parts of the verb, since that word order is always correct.

Ing-Forms as Objects of Two-Word Verbs

Theoretically, of course, any verb that can be followed by a noun object can be followed by an ing-form, since ing-forms can function in most of the ways that nouns can in English sentences. In practice, however, there are only a few two-word verbs that commonly use this construction.

Inseparable Two-Word Verbs

He *insists upon* leaving before daybreak.
Did they *succeed in* learning English?
He doesn't like to *admit to* making a mistake.

If a separable two-word verb has an ing-form as its object, the object almost always *follows* the two parts of the verb.

Separable Two-Word Verbs

Why are you going to *take up* swimming?
He has had to *give up* dancing.
We will *put off* deciding until next week.

Keep on and *go on*, however, when they mean "continue," are always followed by ing-forms. Some grammarians consider these expressions as special auxiliaries, especially *keep*, which can be used without *on*.

The artist *kept on* painting until sunset.
Let's *keep* working until we finish.
Please *go on* playing; don't let me interrupt you.

Nouns Derived from Two-Word Verbs

A great many two-word verbs in English have related noun forms with similar meaning, but with different stress pattern. The nouns are always stressed on the first part, while the verbs are generally stressed on the second part. The base form of the verb is always used in the noun expressions.

The tire *blew out*.	We had a *blowout*.
He likes to *show off*.	He's a *show-off*.
The bank was *held up*.	There was a *holdup* at the bank.
The plane *took off*.	*Take off* is at 9:27 a.m.

Sentences for Practice

A. Practice saying these sentences with two-word verbs in several tenses.

1. They bring up their children carefully.
   They are bringing up their children carefully.
   They brought up their children carefully.
   They will bring up their children carefully.
   They are going to bring up their children carefully.
   They have brought up their children carefully.
   They had brought up their children carefully.
   They should bring up their children carefully.
   They should have brought up their children carefully.

2. Does he get through his work on time?
   Is he getting through his work on time?
   Did he get through his work on time?
   Will he get through his work on time?
   Is he going to get through his work on time?
   Has he gotten through his work on time?
   Had he gotten through his work on time?
   Should he get through his work on time?

3. Don't they talk it over?
   Aren't they talking it over?
   Didn't they talk it over?
   Won't they talk it over?
   Aren't they going to talk it over?
   Haven't they talked it over?
   Hadn't they talked it over?
   Shouldn't they talk it over?
   Shouldn't they have talked it over?

4. The lamp doesn't go out.
   The lamp isn't going out.
   The lamp didn't go out.
   The lamp won't go out.
   The lamp isn't going to go out.
   The lamp hasn't gone out.
   The lamp hadn't gone out.
   The lamp shouldn't go out.
   The lamp shouldn't have gone out.

B. Practice saying these sentences with adverbial modifiers

1. He lives exclusively on vegetables.
   He lives on vegetables exclusively.
2. He broke rudely into our talk.
   He broke into our talk rudely.
3. He waited patiently for the bus.
   He waited for the bus patiently.
4. He counted very much on Donald.
   He counted on Donald very much.
5. He went completely without food.
   He went without food completely.
6. He looked desperately for his wallet.
   He looked for his wallet desperately.
7. He ran accidently into Molly.
   He ran into Molly accidently.
8. He came suddenly across an idea.
   He came across an idea suddenly.
9. He waited politely on the guests.
   He waited on the guests politely.

C. Practice saying these sentences with two-word verbs followed by the ing-form of a verb.

1. Do they insist on leaving?
2. Will they keep on working?
3. Do you feel like studying?
4. Have they succeeded in learning?
5. Did they admit to stealing?
6. Will you take up swimming?
7. Has she given up working?
8. Are you going on traveling?
9. Did she count on winning?
10. Have they held off deciding?

Exercises

A. Add the adverb or adverbial phrase to each sentence in two different positions.

> Example: *thoroughly* The police looked into the matter.
> *The police looked thoroughly into the matter.*
> *The police looked into the matter thoroughly.*

1. *excitedly*   The children got off the bus.
2. *at last*   The parents heard from their son.
3. *quickly*   Let's go over the last ten lessons.
4. *very much*   My brother doesn't care for sports.
5. *hurriedly*   The girls looked for their hats and gloves.
6. *diligently*   Our students keep to their work.
7. *beautifully*   This color goes with black.
8. *briefly*   The lecturer touched on several topics.

B. Change the verbs in the following sentences to the past tense. Use *did* if necessary.

> Example: The children are running away from home.
> *The children ran away from home.*

1. We'll come over for a visit.
2. The committee has seen to the party arrangements.
3. William often tells on his little sister.
4. Those shoes are wearing out too quickly.
5. Why have they torn the building down?
6. When will you put away your things?
7. I haven't figured out those algebra problems.
8. Do green apples disagree with everyone?
9. We haven't got around the difficulties.
10. What will his talk bear on?
11. Why do the tourists insist upon getting off the bus?
12. Who is going to run against Senator Brown?
13. How will the examination turn out?
14. My first impressions are wearing off.

C. Using the longer phrase given beneath each sentence in place of the italicized direct object, rewrite the sentences.

> Example: The wrecking company is tearing *the building* down. (*the large apartment building on Fifteenth Street*)
>
> *The wrecking company is tearing down the large apartment building on Fifteenth Street.*

1. Why did the secretary throw *those letters* away? (*those letters which were signed by the president of the company*)
2. Will the forest rangers be able to put *the fire* out? (*the fire raging in the valley*)
3. This guide book points *the main facts* out. (*the main facts of early American history*)

4. Mrs. Peterson had *an evening dress* on. (*a blue and white silk evening dress*)

5. Have all of the applicants filled *the forms* out? (*forms one, two, three, four, and five*)

6. Only the best students have been able to figure *this problem* out. (*this problem in solid geometry*)

7. They are using dynamite to blow *the ship* up. (*the ship that is being used in that movie about the war*)

8. A baby's teeth are not strong enough to chew *tough foods* up. (*tough foods like meat and uncooked vegetables*)

9. Why did you bring *that subject* up at the meeting? (*that difficult, controversial subject*)

Three-Word Verbs

In order to include another group of rather common verb units, we must modify our definition slightly. There are several two-word verbs which can be followed by nouns only with the addition of a third word, a preposition. These "three-word verbs" are inseparable.

Without an Object	*With an Object*
Look out! A car is coming!	*Look out for* the car!
Please *go on.*	Please *go on with* your work.

Other verbs of this type, with their meanings, are:

	Without Objects	*Inseparable With Objects*
back out	*desert; fail to keep (a promise)*	back out of
bear up	*endure*	bear up under
break in	*interrupt*	break in on
carry on	*continue*	carry on with
catch on	*understand*	catch on to
catch up	*cover the distance between (oneself and a goal)*	catch up with
check out	*leave, pay the bill*	check out of (*leave, e.g., a hotel*)
check up	*investigate*	check up on
come along	*accompany; make progress*	come along with
cut in	*interrupt*	cut in on
drop in	*visit casually without previous planning*	drop in at (on)
drop out	*leave; quit*	drop out of
fall behind	*lag; not progress at the required pace*	fall behind in
fill in	*substitute*	fill in for

57

get ahead	*make progress*	get ahead of (*surpass; beat*)
get along	*have a friendly relationship*	get along with
get away	*escape*	get away with (*do with impunity*)
get by	*manage with difficulty; manage with a minimum of effort*	get by with
go on	*continue*	go on with
hold on	*grasp tightly*	hold on to
hold out	*continue to resist*	hold out against
keep on	*continue*	keep on with
keep up	*maintain the required pace*	keep up with
make out	*progress; succeed*	make out in (with)
run away	*leave; escape*	run away from
talk back	*answer impolitely*	talk back to
wait up	*remain awake in anticipation of something*	wait up for
watch out	*be careful*	watch out for

Sentences for Practice

A. Practice these sentences having three-word verbs followed by objects, and their two-word equivalents without objects. In the first sentence of each pair, make a slight pause between the two function words. In each sentence, stress the word immediately following the verb.

• • ● • • ●	• • ●
1. I got out | of the bus.	I got out.
2. I dropped out | of the course.	I dropped out.
3. I caught on | to the joke.	I caught on.
4. I kept up | with my class.	I kept up.
5. I was through | with the book.	I was through.
6. I filled in | for the teacher.	I filled in.
7. I broke in | on their conversation.	I broke in.

8. I got ahead | of the group.	I got ahead.
9. I fell behind | in my work.	I fell behind.
0. I waited up | for my sister.	I waited up.
1. I checked up | on his record.	I checked up.
2. I held on | to the rope.	I held on.
3. I went on | with my reading.	I went on.
4. I dropped in | on my friend.	I dropped in.

. Practice saying these questions. Stress the last word in
ach sentence.

• · · • ●
1. Why did he talk back?
2. Why did she drop out?
3. Why did you break in?
4. Why did they fall behind?
5. Why did you wait up?
6. Why did she get out?
7. Why did they keep on?
8. Why did he run away?
9. Why did you hold on?
10. Why did you cut in?
11. Why did she back out?
12. Why did you go on?

. Practice saying these questions and answers.
1. What will she keep on with?
   She'll keep on with her work.
2. What will they get by with?
   They'll get by with a little work.
3. What will you hold on to?
   I will hold on to the ropes.
4. What will she catch on to?
   She'll catch on to the dialect.
5. What will he carry on with?
   He'll carry on with his plan.

6. Whom will you fill in for?
   I'll fill in for the chairman.
7. Whom will she wait up for?
   She'll wait up for her daughter.
8. Whom will they get along with?
   They'll get along with each other.
9. Whom will they drop in on?
   They'll drop in on their parents.
10. Whom will they get ahead of?
    They'll get ahead of the others.

Exercises

A. Complete the following sentences by supplying the thir word in the three-word phrase.

1. It is difficult to catch up _____ the fastest runner.
2. Diana is backing out _____ her new responsibilitie
3. Have you decided to keep on _____ your universit courses?
4. Charles got by _____ the least amount of work pos sible!
5. The judge decided to check up _____ the prisoner
6. Mrs. Lewis is bearing up _____ her great sorrow.
7. It's very rude to talk back _____ anyone.
8. In spite of the problem, the engineers are going t carry on _____ the project.
9. Do you like your friends to drop in _____ you with out notice?
10. The news announcer cut in _____ the regular pro gram to announce the election results.
11. How are you coming along _____ your new job?
12. The baby held on _____ her mother's hand.
13. The student nurses aren't making out _____ thei courses too well.

14. You should never break in _____ a private conversation.

15. When Fred was a small boy, he ran away _____ home.

16. Arthur wants to drop out _____ the university.

17. We're trying to keep up _____ the advances of science.

18. Do Mr. Preston and his brother get along _____ each other?

19. Parents often wait up _____ their children.

20. Andrew fell behind _____ his studies and failed the course.

21. Will they be through _____ the equipment soon?

22. Because of the weather, the farmers can't go on _____ their planting.

23. The duty of the vice-president is to fill in _____ the president.

24. I didn't quite catch on _____ what the speaker said.

25. You should always look out _____ the traffic.

B. Give two answers to each of the questions, using first a three-word verb followed by *it*, and then a two-word verb.

1. Are the tourists going to continue their trip?
   Yes, they're going to keep _____ it.
   Yes, they're going to keep _____.

2. Did the doctors examine his medical record?
   Yes, they checked _____ it.
   Yes, they checked _____.

3. Was Mr. Hill able to endure the tragedy?
   Yes, he bore _____ it.
   Yes, he bore _____.

4. Did many of the members leave the club?
   Yes, several did drop _____ it.
   Yes, several did drop _____.

5. Have you ever spoken rudely to your parents?
    Yes, I once talked _____ them.
    Yes, I once talked _____.

6. Are the new teachers succeeding in school?
    Yes, they are getting _____ school.
    Yes, they are getting _____.

7. Have you ever substituted for the director?
    Yes, I've filled _____ him.
    Yes, I've filled _____.

8. Were the girls able to maintain the same pace as the boys?
    Yes, they were able to keep _____ them.
    Yes, they were able to keep _____.

9. Did everyone understand the professor's jokes?
    Yes, they caught _____ them.
    Yes, they caught _____.

C. Complete the answers to each of the following questions, using one of the three-word verbs listed in place of the italicized verb.

back out of	come along with
bear up under	fall behind in
break in on	fill in for
catch on to	keep on with
check up on	make out in

1. Are the business men going to *continue* their advertising campaign:
    No, they aren't going to _____ it.

2. Will the children *accompany* us on our picnic?
    Yes, they'll _____ us.

3. Why did so many students *lag* in their college work?
    They _____ their work because they tried to get by with only a few hours of study.

4. Do you think the new carpenters will *understand* our methods of working?
   I'm sure they will _____ the methods very quickly.

5. Who is going to *substitute* for Mr. Quincy?
   They'll find someone to _____ him.

6. Please don't *interrupt* me when I'm speaking.
   I'm sorry that I _____ you.

7. Do the lawyers intend to *examine* the court proceedings very carefully?
   Yes, they want to _____ the irregularities in the trial.

8. Why did the Representative *fail to keep his promise?*
   He _____ his campaign promises for political reasons.

9. Can the older patients endure the pain as well as the younger ones?
   Some of the older ones _____ pain more easily than the younger patients.

10. Did Frank succeed in his new job in the laboratory?
    Yes, he's _____ the job quite nicely.

LESSON 9

More Three-Word Verbs

Here are some more three-word verbs. Most of them do not have two-word equivalents; they are usually followed by nouns and they are inseparable.

come down with	*become ill with*
come out with	*utter, produce*
come up to	*meet, be equal to*
come up with	*utter, produce*
do away with	*abolish, eliminate*
face up to	*acknowledge* (*something* unpleasant or difficult)
fall back on	*use for emergency purposes*
fall out with	*quarrel with*
feel up to	*feel one has the strength or ability to do* (*something*)
get away with	*do* (*something wrong or unconventional or original*) *without being caught or penalized*
get down to	*become serious about; begin* (*at last*) *to consider*
go back on	*desert; fail to keep* (*a promise*)
go in for	*be interested in, practice*
go through with	*persevere, complete in spite of difficulties*
lie down on	*evade, fail to do* (*one's duty*)
live up to	*maintain* (*a standard*)
look back on	*remember*
look down on	*feel superior to, scorn*
look forward to	*anticipate* (usually *with pleasure*)
look up to	*respect*
make up for	*compensate for*
play up to	*flatter for personal advantage*
put up with	*tolerate*

read up on	*search out information (on a topic) for some special purpose*
run out of	*exhaust the supply of*
stand up for	*support, defend*
stand up to	*resist, remain firm in the face of (opposition or disapproval)*
stick up for	*support, defend*

Sentences for Practice

Practice saying these questions and answers. In each sentence, stress the function word immediately following the verb.

1. Do you look forward | to your vacations?
   Yes, | I look forward to them.
2. Do you stand up | for your country?
   Yes, | I stand up for it.
3. Do you live up | to your ideals?
   Yes, | I live up to them.
4. Do you put up | with his nonsense?
   Yes, | I put up with it.
5. Do you face up | to the facts?
   Yes, | I face up to them.
6. Do you stick up | for your rights?
   Yes, | I stick up for them.
7. Do you feel up | to the job?
   Yes, | I feel up to it.
8. Do you look back | on the past?
   Yes, | I look back on it.
9. Did he go back | on his word?
   Yes, | he went back on it.
10. Do you play up | to your boss?
    Yes, | I play up to him.

Exercises

A. Rewrite the following sentences by substituting a three-word verb for the italicized verb.

1. Children should *respect* their parents.
2. Parents should not *scorn* their children.
3. It isn't easy to *tolerate* people who are impolite.
4. We should all *support* the things in which we believe.
5. Doris *uttered* a very strange comment last night.
6. Are the guides going to *accompany* us all day?
7. Many people think we should *abolish* boxing.
8. Sometimes it's pleasant to *remember* one's childhood.
9. I don't like people who try to *flatter* me.
10. Let's *be definite about* the facts.

B. Complete the following sentences by writing in the proper function words. The meanings are given at the left of each sentence.

1. *disrespect*   Do you look _____ anyone?
2. *anticipate*   Most people look _____ their vacations.
3. *share*   I've lost my book. May I look _____ you?
4. *be careful*   When you're walking in the woods, look _____ poison ivy.
5. *respect*   The public should be able to look _____ its leaders.
6. *remember*   Jackson looks _____ his failure with regret.
7. *feel superior*   Why do some people insist on looking _____ others?

C. Complete the three-word verb in these sentences.

1. Will you be able to get by _____ a small salary in New York?
2. When the passengers got out _____ the plane, they hurried to the waiting room.

3. Not many criminals get away _____ their crimes.
4. Robert worked hard so that he could get ahead _____ the others.
5. After the beginning experiments, we'll have to get down _____ more complicated problems.
6. The great leaders of the world have always stood up _____ their principles.
7. Don't let people pick on you; just stand up _____ them.
8. The engineers are going through _____ their highway project, even though the expenses have risen.
9. If you want to be trusted, you should never go back _____ your word.
10. Joseph is a natural comedian; he's always coming out _____ humorous remarks.
11. Mrs. Nelson came down _____ pneumonia and was taken to the hospital.
12. If these new methods don't work, we'll have to fall back _____ our old system.
13. We will continue to live up _____ our promises.
14. I will not put up _____ his laxness any longer!
15. The store had run out _____ shoes in his size.
16. Please read up _____ this political theory before the next class.
17. Gordon has never been able to face up _____ the realities of life.
18. Laura has a cold and doesn't feel up _____ working today.
19. If Edward keeps lying down _____ the job, he'll soon be fired.
20. Wasn't there anyone who would stick up _____ Howard's proposals?
21. This department isn't profitable; we'll have to do away _____ it.
22. The manager will have to hire two people to make up _____ the lost time.

D. Write answers to these questions, using a three-word verb in place of the italicized verb. Use the words in parentheses as the direct object.

> Example: Whom should children *respect?* (*their parents and teachers*)
>
> *Children should look up to their parents and teachers.*

1. What are the boys and girls *anticipating?* (*a trip to the beach*)
2. Which policy is Fuller *supporting?* (*the independent policy*)
3. What hobbies *are* your sons *interested in?* (*stamp collecting and photography*)
4. Which office machines are you going to *eliminate?* (*the old typewriters*)
5. Which student did Lawrence *quarrel* with? (*Tom*)
6. What promise did the Congressman *fail to keep?* (*his promise to support a decrease in taxes*)
7. Whom did little Billy *answer* rudely? (*his Aunt Dorothy*)

Two-Word Verbs With More Than One Meaning

In previous lessons we learned that some two-word verbs can have more than one usage; that is, some verbs may occur either with or without objects. There are complications with other two-word verbs in still another way: some of these verbs have more than one meaning in addition to having more than one usage. The construction *pass on*, for example, can be separable or inseparable, and it can occur with and without an object, and each usage has a meaning that is different from that of the normal verb + prepositional phrase construction.

separable:	Did they *pass on* the information to the newspaper? (*transmit*)
inseparable with an object:	Congress hasn't *passed on* the resolution yet. (*made a decision*)
inseparable without an object:	Mrs. Taber *passed on* last night at the age of 89. (*died*)
verb + prepositional phrase:	Our cars *passed* on the highway.

Furthermore, there are other verb combinations which have two or more meanings for the same form with the same usage. *Make up* as a separable verb, for example, has four possible meanings.

> Uncle Dick *made up* an interesting story for the children. (*invented*)

> I haven't *made up* my shopping list yet. (*composed; written*)

Because you were ill, you'll have to *make up* the final exam. (*complete what was missed*)

Alice *made up* her face for her part in the play. (*applied cosmetics*)

And *make up* has still another meaning with or without an object.

Paul and his brother had a terrible quarrel, but they apologized and *made up*. (*became reconciled*)

They *made up* their quarrel.

A list follows of two-word verbs presented in earlier lessons which have meanings in addition to those first given. As a partial review of the previous lessons, both the old and the new meanings are presented, along with illustrations of the different usages. The designation (inf.) indicates those usages that are informal.

Separable Verbs

back up 1. *cause to move backwards*; 2. *support*

blow up *cause to explode, destroy by explosives*

break down 1. *analyze*; 2. *list separately*

break up 1. *break into small pieces*; 2. *stop (a fight)*

brush off 1. *brush the surface of;* 2. *snub, dismiss without courtesy* (inf.)

Inseparable Verbs, With Objects

call for 1. *come to get*; 2. *require* (as a law, recipe, etc.)

Inseparable Verbs, Without Objects

back up *move backwards*

blow up 1. *explode*; 2. *become suddenly angry, lose one's temper* (inf.)

break down 1. *stop operating properly*; 2. *become ill to the point of incapacity*

break up 1. *break into small pieces*; 2. *disperse* (of a group, meeting, etc.); 3. *cease associating* (as a married couple, group of friends, etc.)

71

Separable Verbs	Inseparable Verbs, With Objects	Inseparable Verbs, Without Objects
call off 1. *cancel* (*something scheduled*); 2. *order away* (*attacking dogs, troops, etc.*)		
	call on 1. *visit;* 2. *ask to speak, serve, etc.;* 3. *appeal to for help*	
call up 1. *telephone;* 2. *summon for compulsory military service*		**call up** *telephone* (inf.)
	care for 1. *like;* 2. *tend, guard, supervise*	
carry on *continue*		**carry on** 1. *continue as before;* 2. *misbehave* (inf.)
cheer up *cause to become cheerful*		**cheer up** *become cheerful*
	come across with *yield or produce* (*something demanded*) (inf.)	**come across** *yield* (inf.)
	come along with *accompany*	**come along** *make progress*
	get around *avoid, evade*	**get around** *circulate, move about* (inf.)

72

get off *send, dispatch; succeed in removing*

get on *don, put on*

get up *cause to rise*

hold off *restrain*

get off *leave (a public vehicle, a platform, etc.); dismount*

get on *enter (a public vehicle), mount*

get on/along with *be compatible with*

get through (with) *terminate, finish*

go with 1. *harmonize with;* 2. *accompany (a person of the opposite sex) regularly in public, for courtship*

hang around *remain idly in the vicinity of* (inf.)

hold on to *grasp firmly*

get off *leave*

get on *mount*

get on/along 1. *progress;* 2. *be compatible;* 3. *grow old* (inf.)

get through *finish*

get up *rise* (from a sitting or reclining position)

hang around *remain idly, dawdle* (inf.)

hold off *postpone* (an action)

hold on 1. *support oneself by grasping with the hands;* 2. *persevere;* 3. *wait while telephoning* (inf.)

Separable Verbs	Inseparable Verbs, With Objects	Inseparable Verbs, Without Objects
look up 1. *seek* (*information*) *in a reference book;* 2. *locate and visit*	**look for** 1. *seek;* 2. *expect* (inf.)	
make out 1. *understand, with difficulty;* 2. *decipher*		**make out** *succeed, progress* (inf.)
mix up 1. *mingle thoroughly;* 2. *confuse*		
pick up 1. *take up with the fingers or in a similar manner;* 2. *come to meet and escort* (*someone*); 3. *learn, casually and without particular effort;* 4. *initiate an association with someone in public, often not under respectable circumstances*		**pick up** *grow, increase* (inf.)

74

put on 1. *dress in;* 2. *initiate the operation of*

put out *inconvenience (someone)*

run away *leave quickly without permission or authorization, escape*

run into 1. *collide with;* 2. *encounter accidentally* (inf.)

run off 1. *drive away;* 2. *make multiple copies of, by machine*

run off *drain* (of water)

run over *hit with a vehicle*

run over *go to visit casually* (inf.)

show up *prove (someone) to be wrong, dishonest, etc.* (inf.)

show up *appear, arrive* (inf.; this expression is pejorative in its connotations)

shut up *force to be quiet* (very inf.; to be avoided)

shut up *be quiet* (an insulting expression when used as a command; to be avoided)

stand up *fail to keep an appointment with* (inf.)

stand up 1. *rise from a sitting position;* 2. *endure under conditions of stress*

Separable Verbs

take off 1. *remove; 2. satirize, ridicule; 3. take (an amount of time) as leave* (said of employees)

take up 1. *study, prepare for a career in; 2. consider at a public meeting; 3. discuss; 4. shorten (a garment); 5. continue from a point previously reached*

turn on *start the operation of*

turn out 1. *produce; 2. dismiss (someone from the place where he usually lives), force into exile*

wear out 1. *use (something) until it is no longer usable; 2. tire greatly, exhaust the strength of*

Inseparable Verbs, With Objects

turn on *attack unexpectedly*

Inseparable Verbs, Without Objects

take off 1. *leave the ground (of aircraft); 2. not report for work* (said of employees)

turn out *prove to be, succeed* (often followed by adverbs)

wear out *become used up, no longer serviceable*

Sentences for Practice

A. Practice saying these sentences.

1. Will you back me up?
2. Did you break it down?
3. Have they broken it up?
4. Did she brush you off?
5. Did they call him up?
6. Will you get it off?
7. Can she get it on?
8. Did they get it through?
9. Did he stand her up?
10. Have they taken it up?
11. Will they turn her out?
12. Did it tire him out?

B. Practice saying these sentences.

1. We backed up the car.
   We backed up the theory.
   We backed up into the driveway.
2. They broke down the formula.
   The machine broke down.
   Mrs. Carter broke down.
3. She broke up the candy.
   The classes broke up.
   They broke up the meeting.
4. I called him up.
   John called up last night.
   The army called him up.
5. He carried on his work.
   He carried on diligently.
   He carried on.
6. She got on her clothes.
   She got on the bus.
   She got on quite well.

7. He picked the paper up.
   Business picked up.
   He picked up the language.
8. They took off their coats.
   They took off six days.
   The plane took off.
9. The meeting turned out a success.
   The factory turned out tractors.
   The hotel turned them out.

Exercises

A. Complete the following pairs of sentences with two-word verbs. Use the same two-word verb for both sentences in each pair.

1. *summon to military service*

   Will Harold be _____ before he goes to college?

   telephone

   Please _____ me _____ when you find out the news.

2. *seek*

   What are the girls _____?

   expect

   We didn't _____ the visitors until after midnight.

3. *stop operating*

   My radio has _____ again.

   become ill and exhausted

   David _____ because of overwork and worry.

4. *explode*

   The gasoline truck _____ when it ran into the tree.

   become angry

   It was very embarrassing when Mr. Schuman _____ at the office yesterday.

5. *arise suddenly*

   The epidemic _____ in the early part of January.

   develop spots

   Clara's face _____ when she became ill.

6. *understand*   Can you _____ what this letter
                     means?

    succeed   How did the new students _____?

7. *drive backwards* Can the engineer _____ the
                       train?

    support   The committee members _____
                     the director's decision.

8. *seek in a*   They had to _____ the location
    reference   of the river in an atlas.
    book
    locate and   Please _____ me _____ when
    visit   you come to the city again.

9. *brush the surface* Don't forget to _____ your coat.

    ignore   Why did Mary _____ that new
                     boy last night when he asked
                     her to dance?

10. *visit*   The students are invited to _____
                     their professors at their homes.

    appeal to   The Red Cross will _____ the
                     public for contributions during
                     the disaster.

11. *meet and escort* Ralph is going to _____ us
                       _____ before the concert.

    increase   The production at that factory
                     has _____ thirty percent.

12. *prove to be*   Martha was sure she was right,
    wrong   but Jane _____ her _____.
    appear   Only a few people _____ at his
                     recital.

13. *shorten*   The dress is too long, so she'll
                     have to _____ it _____.

    consider   The city council will _____ the
                     transportation problem.

14. *confuse*   The tourists were very _____ when they arrived.

    mix completely   Be sure to _____ the ingredients thoroughly before you bake this cake.

15. *start*   The heat in the apartment building is usually _____ in October.

    clothe oneself in   What are the girls going to _____ for the dance?

B. Complete the answers to the following sentences by using one of the following two-word verbs: **break down, break out,** or **break up.**

1. Have the chemists analyzed that substance? Yes, they have _____ it _____ into its basic elements.

2. Why was Dan so upset? He _____ when he heard about the accident.

3. What time did the meeting stop? It _____ at about 11:30.

4. Have all of the electric typewriters stopped working? Yes, every one of them has _____.

5. Do they think another war will take place? Everyone hopes that another war will not _____.

6. Does this newspaper analyze the news? Yes, they _____ the news _____ into several categories.

7. What is the matter with Arthur's face? He has the measles, and spots have _____ all over his body, too.

8. Why did the class stop so early? It _____ because a special lecture was scheduled at 11 o'clock.

9. Is Mrs. Gibbs upset? Yes, she has been working too hard and has _____ completely.

10. Why did the riots occur? The riots _____ because of unemployment problems.

C. Complete these sentences with the correct function word, the meaning of which is given at the left of each sentence.

1. *finish*   The electricians will get _____ the wiring early next month.

2. *send*   Please get these airmail letters _____ before the regular mail.

3. *dress oneself in*   It takes the children a long time to get their winter clothes _____.

4. *evade*   Some taxpayers try to get _____ the regulations so they won't have to pay taxes.

5. *rise*   On holidays, we don't have to get _____ so early.

6. *enter, leave*   We should get _____ the bus at the station and get _____ near the university.

7. *circulate*   Irving certainly does get _____ a lot, doesn't he?

8. *cause to rise*   Don't forget to get the children _____ in time to go to school.

9. *avoid*   The architects have been unable to get _____ the problem of a shortage of building materials.

10. *send*   We will go to the telegraph office and get the message _____ as quickly as possible.

LESSON 11

Two-Word Verbs and Vocabulary Study

After one masters the structural problems presented in the previous lessons, the study of two-word verbs becomes primarily a problem of vocabulary. The list of two-word verbs is quite long, and, like most other groups of idiomatic expressions, is constantly being changed. During any given period of time, one may hear dozens of new two-word verb combinations. Some of them, after a while, will disappear from active usage. Others will be retained and become permanent vocabulary items. This, of course, presents a problem in the making of verb lists. Should one, for example, include a two-word verb such as *put on,* meaning "deceive or fool," which was popular in the 1960's? This particular two-word verb may prove to be only a passing slang expression; on the other hand, it may become a part of the standard vocabulary.

The lists in these final lessons are composed of verb units that seem to be fairly well-established in the language. Some of them are primarily informal in usage, but all are common in the speech of the average speaker of American English.

The following are additional examples of separable two-word verbs:

break in	*use (something new) until it is comfortable; use (a new machine,* such as a *car) in a special way at first; train (a horse)*
break into	*go into a house or room forcibly; suddenly begin* (as laughter, song)
bring out	*publish; emphasize; set at ease*
bring to	*restore to consciousness*
buy out	*buy the other person's share* in a jointly-owned business

82

buy up	*buy the whole supply of (a kind of merchandise)*
carry out	*accomplish, perform, execute (a plan, order,* etc.*)*
count in	*include*
count out	*exclude*
count up	*add to a total*
cut off	*interrupt*
draw up	*write, compose (a document)*
figure up	*compute*
give away	*give (indiscriminately, as something one no longer wants); betray (a secret, a trust)*
hand in	*submit, present*
have over	*entertain informally (at home)*
hold up	*delay; rob,* threatening the victim with a gun or other weapon
pan out	*turn out well, be successful*
put across	*cause to be understood or accepted*
see off	*accompany someone to the beginning of a trip:* e.g., to a ship or a train
see through	*complete* in spite of difficulties
set up	*arrange*
spell out	*enumerate in detail*
think through	*consider something from beginning to end*
tire out	*cause to be exhausted*
turn down	*refuse; lower the volume (of a radio,* etc.*)*
turn in	*submit, deliver*
turn up	*appear, arrive unexpectedly or off schedule (= show up)*
write down	*record*
write out	*write down every detail of*

Sentences for Practice

A. Practice saying these sentences, putting the loud stress on the last word.

1. He wrote down the word. He wrote it down.
2. He tired out the boys. He tired them out.
3. I turned in my lesson. I turned it in.
4. She handed in her work. She handed it in.
5. They shut off the motor. They shut it off.
6. You cut off the speaker. You cut him off.
7. He turned down the job. He turned it down.
8. We held up the meeting. We held it up.
9. I crossed out the names. I crossed them out.
10. She thought through the problem. She thought it through.

B. Practice saying these questions and answers.

1. Did he carry out the plans?
   Yes, he carried them out.
2. Did you draw up a contract?
   Yes, I drew one up.
3. Did she cheer up the patients?
   Yes, she cheered them up.
4. Will he bring out a book?
   Yes, he will bring one out.
5. Did they buy up the supplies?
   Yes, they bought them up.
6. Did he buy out his brother?
   Yes, he bought him out.
7. Has she broken in the shoes?
   Yes, she has broken them in.

8. Did I blow out the match?
   Yes, you blew it out.
9. Will she give away the ring?
   Yes, she will give it away.
10. Did I put across the idea?
    Yes, you put it across.
11. Has he carried out the project?
    Yes, he has carried it out.
12. Did they figure up the costs?
    Yes, they figured them up.
13. Will she set up an appointment?
    Yes, she will set one up.
14. Are we counting in the Smiths?
    Yes, we're counting them in.

Exercises

A. Change the italicized object in the sentences below to a personal pronoun, changing the word order if necessary.

1. Why hasn't Richard handed in *his report?*
2. The employer turned down *the Leonard man* because of his poor health.
3. The court stenographer wrote down *everything that was said.*
4. How many thieves held up *the bank?*
5. Don't make a decision until you think through *the whole problem.*
6. Their first day at the beach tired *the children* out.
7. When is the publishing company going to bring out *Henry's book?*
8. Please turn in *your assignment* before you leave the classroom.
9. The storm cut off *all the electricity in the county.*

10. Did you manage to cheer up *your parents* when you talked to them?
11. The ABC company has bought out *the XYZ company*.
12. It isn't always easy to break in *new shoes*.
13. Let's go down to the ship and see the *Lawsons* off.
14. It won't take long to figure up *the expenses*.
15. The board of directors is going to draw up *the new contract*.

B. Complete the answers to these questions by adding the proper function word.

1. Who is publishing John's book? The Wilkins Publishing Co. is going to bring it _____.
2. Why did you leave Peter off the list? Because Peter asked us to count him _____.
3. Why are you so determined to complete the project? We promised to see it _____ before the end of the year.
4. What is delaying the beginning of the concert? I don't know what is holding it _____.
5. Why are you so exhausted? Painting the house tired me _____.
6. Do we have to record everything that is said? Yes, we should write everything _____.
7. Why was Lawrence refused by the Navy? He was turned _____ because he was too young.
8. Should we include Mr. and Mrs. Burns on our list? Yes, we can count them _____.
9. How many items were deleted from the list of supplies? They crossed _____ ten different items.
10. Who is going to arrange the program? Teresa is supposed to set it _____.

C. Fill in the blank with the correct function word to complete the two-word verb, the meaning of which is given at the left of each sentence.

1. *submit*   The teachers have to turn _____ their reports at the end of the school year.

2. *refuse*   This suggestion was turned _____ because of its impracticality.

3. *appear*   Do you think many people will turn _____ at the performance?

4. *start*   Please don't turn _____ the radio until five o'clock.

5. *stop*   The children turned the TV _____ after watching their favorite show.

6. *publish*   Mary hasn't found anyone to bring _____ her novel.

7. *raise*   Thomas is going to bring _____ that question at the meeting tonight.

8. *cause*   Scientists say that many factors bring _____ changes in the weather.

9. *raise*   Mr. Miller has brought _____ seven sons.

10. *postpone*   The housing development was put _____ because of the increased expenses.

11. *dress oneself in*   You need to put _____ something warmer than a jacket.

12. *extinguish*   The wind suddenly put _____ the candle.

13. *cause to be accepted*   Bill couldn't put his ideas _____ at all.

14. *store*   Children have to learn to put their things _____.

D. Complete these sentences by writing in the proper verb.

1. *delay*   How many times has that meeting been _____ up?

2. *compose*   The regulations were _____ up by the new management.

3. *purchase in large quantities*   The new factory will have to _____ up a large supply of chemicals.

4. *cause to be cheerful*   The news _____ us up greatly.

5. *arrange*   The entertainment committee has already _____ up the dance.

6. *compute*   You should _____ up your expenses before you leave.

7. *fail to meet*   Why did Nancy _____ Bill up last night?

8. *confuse*   The directions weren't clear, so everyone was all _____ up.

9. *diminish*   The storm _____ up late in the evening.

More Separable Verbs

Of the three types of two-word verbs (separable, inseparable with objects, and inseparable without objects) the largest group seems to be the separable group. In addition to those already presented, other common verb units of this type are:

break off	*end, stop abruptly*
bring off	*accomplish (something difficult or unexpected)*
bring on	*cause*
cut down	*reduce in quantity*
cut out	*eliminate, delete*
get across	*cause to be understood*
give off	*emit*
hand down	*deliver, pronounce formally (in court); leave as an inheritance*
hand out	*distribute*
hand over	*yield control of*
let down	*disappoint; make longer (in sewing)*
let out	*release from confinement; make larger (in sewing)*
play down	*minimize, not give a great deal of emphasis to*
rule out	*eliminate*
take in	*understand (something); fool, deceive (someone); make smaller (in sewing)*
take out	*escort on a social date; remove*
think up	*create, invent*
touch up	*repair; add finishing touches to*
use up	*use all of*
wind up	*finish, bring to a close*

Sentences for Practice

A. Practice saying these sentences.

1. What did he think up?   He thought up a good answer.
2. What did he touch up?   He touched up the painting.
3. What did he use up?   He used up the salt.
4. What did he break off?   He broke off the engagement.
5. What did he bring off?   He brought off the event.
6. What did he get across?   He got across the idea.
7. What did he give away?   He gave away a pen.
8. What did he cut out?   He cut out smoking.
9. What did he hand down?   He handed down the decision.
10. What did he hand out?   He handed out the papers.

B. Practice saying these sentences. Notice the stress pattern.

1. Who revealed it?   Bob gave it away.
2. Who created it?   Anne thought it up.
3. Who finished it?   The boys wound it up.
4. What caused it?   The war brought it on.
5. Who accomplished it?   The women brought it off.
6. Who distributed it?   The farmers handed it out.
7. Who repaired it?   The artist touched it up.
8. Who ended it?   Peter broke it off.
9. Who reduced it?   William cut it down.
10. Who continued it?   The men carried it on.

Exercises

A. Change the word order to the separable pattern, using a pronoun for the italicized words.

> Example: We had to rule out *the possibility of increased supplies.*
>
> *We had to rule it out.*

1. Why did the press play down *the story about the border disturbance?*
2. Joan's dressmaker had to let down *all of her skirts.*
3. The children will have to cut down *their playtime hours* when school opens.
4. Let's wind up *the plans* tonight after dinner.
5. Please ask Harry to hand out *the papers.*
6. Why did Dick give away *his fountain pen?*
7. William let *his parents* down by not accepting the scholarship.
8. No one was able to get across *the theory* to the class.
9. When will the owners hand over *the property* to the buyers?
10. Please take in *the waist of this dress* a little.
11. I'll have to let out *the coat* before I can wear it.
12. Who thought up *that fantastic idea?*

B. Complete these sentences by using one of the listed two-word verbs.

give away	hand down	take in
give back	hand in	take off
give in	hand out	take out
give off	hand over	take up

1. *remove*   The children had to _____ their wet clothes.
2. *distribute*   The rescue workers _____ supplies to the victims of the earthquake.
3. *submit*   You must _____ your report before the end of this month.

4. *emitted* That fertilizer factory _____ an unpleasant smell.

5. *present as a gift* Mrs. Lyons is always _____ things to her friends.

6. *escort* Who is _____ Della _____ tonight?

7. *pronounce* The judges _____ their decisions every Monday.

8. *yield control of* We will _____ the documents after we receive the payments.

9. *make smaller* She had to _____ the dress a few inches at the waist.

10. *reveal* Please don't _____ this information to anyone.

11. *relent* If Ronald does his work well, perhaps his parents will _____ and buy him a bicycle.

12. *study* What is Clarence going to _____ at college?

13. *return* When will the Carsons have to _____ the money _____ to the bank?

14. *deceive* Both Mr. Mills and his wife were _____ by that smooth-talking salesman.

C. Rewrite each of the following sentences by substituting the phrase in parentheses for the italicized personal pronoun. Put the phrase after the function word.

> Example: Barbara will have to take *it* in. (*her new dress*)
>
> Barbara will have to take in her new dress.

1. Did Paul take *her* out last night? (*his new girl friend*)
2. We'll have to touch *it* up before we sell it. (*the antique chair*)
3. Have the carpenters used *them* up? (*the floor boards*)
4. Did the amateur actors bring *it* off? (*the special performance*)

5. Are the doctors carrying *it* over? (*the medical conference*)
6. The federal court will hand *it* down next month. (*the final decision*)
7. The television reporters played *it* down. (*the unexpected result*)
8. The decision was to rule *it* out. (*the last suggestion*)
9. Why did they have to cut *it* out? (*the last half*)

D. Complete the following sentences by using one of the two-word verbs on the list. The meaning is given by the word to the left of each sentence.

carry over	have over
do over	look over
get over	put over
go over	run over
hand over	talk over

1. *review*   Let's _____ Lessons 1 through 10.
2. *examine*   Please _____ your paper carefully.
3. *continue*   Because of the public interest, the lectures will be _____ for another week.
4. *discuss*   Edward is going to _____ the problem _____ with his advisor.
5. *recover from*   Miss Black _____ her illness very slowly.
6. *invite to visit*   I'd like to _____ everyone in the office _____ for a dinner party next week.
7. *yield control of*   The former mayor _____ his authority _____ to his successor the day after the elections.
8. *cause to be understood*   David _____ the central point of his lecture very well.
9. *redo*   Do we have to _____ the entire lesson _____?
10. *hit with a car*   The car _____ Mrs. Becker and seriously injured her.

LESSON 13

Separable Verbs That Also Occur Without Objects

As we noted in an earlier lesson, there are many two-word verbs that occur both with and without objects, keeping the same general meaning. Those listed below belong to this category.

calm down	*become calm; cause to be calm*
close down	*close permanently*
close up	*close temporarily*
give up	*surrender*
keep up	*continue, keep the same pace; maintain*
quiet down	*be quiet; cause to be quiet*
save up	*accumulate*
sell out	*sell the ownership* (of a business)
slow down	*go more slowly; cause to go more slowly*
slow up	*go more slowly; cause to go more slowly*
take over	*assume command of*
work out	*be successful; solve*

There are other separable verbs which appear without objects, but which then have different meanings. Strictly speaking, such verbs as these are two different verbs, not a single verb with two meanings.

Verb	*Meaning with object*	*Meaning without an object*
clear up	*clarify; tidy*	*become clear*
give out	*distribute; announce*	*become exhausted*
give up	*surrender* (something)	*surrender; fail to finish*
make out	*perceive with difficulty; write* (a check, document, etc.)	*succeed*

pass out	*distribute*	*become unconscious*
run down	*trace;*	*slowly lose power so*
	disparage;	*as to stop function-*
	hit with a vehicle	*ing,* as a clock
turn in	*submit; deliver*	*go to bed*
turn out	*produce; extinguish*	*come; appear end,*
	(a light); force to	*conclude*
	leave	

Sentences for Practice

A. Practice saying the following sentences.

1. Should we save up the money?
     Yes, save it up.
     All right, we'll save up.
2. Should we take the business over?
     Yes, take it over.
     All right, we'll take over.
3. Should we keep up the work despite the rain?
     Yes, keep it up, even if the rain keeps up.*
4. Should we sell out the company?
     Yes, sell it out.
     All right, we'll sell out.
5. Should we close up the office?
     Yes, close it up.
     All right, we'll close up.
6. Should we slow down the car?
     Yes, slow it down.
     All right, we'll slow down.

B. Practice saying these sentences.

1. She distributed the books.
     She passed them out.
2. She became unconscious.
     She passed out.

  * This verb is not generally used both with and without an object
after the same subject. *Persons* can keep up a *thing;* a *thing* can
keep up.

3. They clarified the problem.
   They cleared it up.
4. The weather improved.
   It cleared up.
5. I understood the handwriting.
   I made it out.
6. I succeeded.
   I made out well.
7. They extinguished the light.
   They turned it out.
8. A large crowd came.
   A large crowd turned out.
9. He delivered the report.
   He turned it in.
10. He went to bed early.
    He turned in early.
11. He announced the news.
    He gave out the news.
12. He became exhausted.
    He gave out.
13. We traced the story to its origin.
    We ran down the story.
14. Your watch stopped running.
    Your watch ran down.

Exercises

A. Complete these sentences by using one of the two-word verbs listed below. Meanings are given at the left of each sentence.

break down	give up	run down
clear up	make out	turn in
give out	pass out	turn out

1. *succeed*   The farmers _____ very well with their crops last year.

2. *deliver*   When are the supervisors going to _____ their reports _____?

3. *become exhausted*   Several of the long distance runners _____ before the end of the race.

4. *trace*   I'm not sure of the date of this event; I'll have to _____ it _____ at the library.

5. *disparage*   Why does Joseph always _____ his family _____ when he talks about them?

6. *become unconscious*   Lola _____ when she heard the news.

7. *fail to finish*   I _____ when I saw that I was losing the game.

8. *clarify*   We need an expert to _____ this theoretical problem.

9. *hit with a vehicle*   Arthur was _____ by an unoccupied automobile whose brakes had failed.

10. *go to bed*   What time do you usually _____?

11. *distribute*   The salesmen are _____ samples of their products among the housewives.

12. *improve*   The atmosphere has _____ considerably.

13. *stop operating*   Why did the vacuum cleaner _____ so soon after we bought it?

14. *understand*   The telephone connection was bad and I couldn't _____ what he was saying to me.

15. *surrender*   The soldiers _____ when they saw that they were surrounded.

16. *result*   The program didn't _____ very well after all.

17. *produce*   This machine can _____ more than one hundred copies a minute.

B. Give affirmative answers to these questions, using the italicized verb without an object.

> Example: Is George trying to *cut* his weight *down?*
> *Yes, he's trying to cut down.*

1. Have you *saved up* a lot of money? Yes, _____.
2. Will the new administrative officers *take over* the company immediately? Yes, _____.
3. Did the baseball players *keep up* their lead? Yes, _____.
4. Are the Sawyers going to *close* their grocery store *down?* Yes, _____.
5. Did Dr. Miller *close up* his office early today? Yes, _____.
6. Did the driver *slow* the bus *down?* Yes, _____.
7. Is Mr. Underwood going to *give up* looking for a job? Yes, _____.

C. Complete the answers to these questions by using a two-word verb with the same meaning as the italicized verb.

1. Why is Mr. Jones *reducing* his supply of spare parts? He is _____ the supply because there is no storage space.
2. How much money have you *accumulated* from your summer job? I've _____ nearly two hundred dollars.
3. Will Mr. Chase *assume control of* the company? Yes, he'll _____ it _____ a few weeks from now.
4. Was Diana able to *continue* her studying? No, she wasn't able to _____ it _____.
5. Can Jim *make* the boys *be quiet?* He's trying to _____ them _____ right now.
6. Why did Roland *surrender* the game so quickly? He _____ because he realized that he was defeated.

7. Did Edna *become unconscious* because of the heat?
   Yes, she _____ when the temperature went up to ninety-nine degrees.
8. Who will *clarify* this misunderstanding?
   Mr. Lewis should be able to _____ it _____.
9. Which factory *produces* the most?
   The new factory _____ more than the old factory.

D. Complete the following sentences with one of the two-word verbs listed below.

turn around	turn on
turn down	turn out
turn in	turn up
turn off	

1. *appear*   How many tourists _____ for the guided tour through the museum?
2. *go to bed*   I'm going to _____ early tonight.
3. *refuse*   Sam's application was _____ because of his poor employment record.
4. *result*   Why didn't the entertainment _____ well this time?
5. *extinguish* This lamp has to be _____ at midnight.
6. *start*   Let's _____ the radio _____ while we're washing the dishes.
7. *produce*   Steven has _____ a new book every year for ten years.
8. *deliver*   Our papers have to be _____ one week before the examination.
9. *stop the operation of*   You have to _____ the motor of the car while gas is being put in.
10. *reverse*   The bus is too large to _____ in this narrow street.

E. Complete the following sentences by choosing the correct function word.

1. *meet*
   accidentally

   I ran _____ my former employer last week.

2. *campaign*
   against

   Who is going to run _____ Senator Jones?

3. *collide with*

   The driver lost control of the bus and ran _____ a tree.

4. *hit with*
   a car

   Was it a drunken driver who ran _____ the little boys?

5. *escape*

   When Henry was a small boy, he wanted to run _____.

6. *find*
   accidentally

   Where did you run _____ that unusual theory?

7. *campaign for*

   Mr. Williams wants to run _____ governor of the state.

8. *hit with*
   a car

   It was dark when we ran _____ the dog.

9. *force to*
   leave

   Farmers often have to run _____ wild animals from their fields.

10. *meet*
    accidentally

    Do you often run _____ the other members of your old club?

More Two-Word Verbs Without Objects

The following are common two-word verbs that do not have objects:

blow in	*drop in to visit unexpectedly* (slang)
blow over	*pass without doing harm*
come by	*visit*
come out	*appear; make a social debut*
come through	*succeed* (in spite of difficulties)
come to	*regain consciousness*
die away	*fade, diminish*
die down	*fade, diminish*
die off/out	*disappear, become extinct*
fall off	*decrease*
go on	*happen*
go over	*succeed*
grow up	*mature*
hold out	*persevere; persist*
pull in	*arrive* (of a vehicle)
pull out	*depart* (of a vehicle)
pull through	*survive*
stand by	*wait; be prepared to assist*
stand out	*be noticeable; excel*
stand up	*last, endure*

Sentences for Practice

A. Practice saying these sentences, putting the loud stress on the last word.

1. The noise died down.
2. The sounds died away.
3. The tribe died off.
4. The plants died out.

101

5. The train pulled in.
6. The bus pulled out.
7. The patient pulled through.
8. The leaders stand out.
9. The assistants stood by.
10. The storm blew over.
11. The child grew up.
12. The car stood up.
13. The army held out.
14. The sun came out.
15. The patient came to.
16. A friend came along.

B. Practice saying these questions and answers.

1. What did Ken do?	He came out.
2. What did Dick do?	He came along.
3. What did Tom do?	He came, too.
4. What did Bill do?	He came by.
5. What did Charles do?	He came through.

Exercises

A. Complete the answers to the questions by using the proper function word.

1. When did the storm begin to fade?
   It started to die _____ shortly before midnight.
2. Why did that race of animals disappear?
   It died _____ because it was unable to adapt to changing conditions.
3. Did you invite the Bensons to visit us?
   Yes, they're going to come _____ next Sunday.
4. How did the charity drive succeed?
   I think it went _____ very well.
5. What time does the morning edition of the paper appear?
   It comes _____ at four a.m.

6. What happened?
   Something very strange is going _____ down at the corner.
7. Does the weatherman say the storm will pass without doing much damage?
   Yes, it will probably blow _____.
8. How long did your first car last?
   It stood _____ for more than ten years.
9. Who is the outstanding literary figure today?
   There are many poets, dramatists, and novelists who stand _____.
10. Has the bus arrived yet?
    Yes, it pulled _____ a few minutes ago.
11. Is the patient conscious now?
    No, he hasn't come _____ yet.
12. Do you think our school team will do well in the tournament?
    Yes, it should come _____ very well.
13. How long have the assistants been waiting?
    They have been standing _____ since ten o'clock.
14. Will all of the injured men survive?
    The doctor thinks everyone will pull _____.

B. Rewrite the following sentences by replacing the italicized expression with the proper form of a two- (or three-) word verb with go.

> Example: No one trusts Philip because he *doesn't keep* his word.
>
> > No one trusts Philip because he goes back on *his word*.

1. What colors *harmonize with* blue and green?
2. The lights *are* often *extinguished* during bad storms.
3. When will Mr. and Mrs. Baldwin *return* to Wichita?
4. The photographer *continued* his picture-taking in spite of the rain.
5. Will someone please tell me what is *happening*?

6. The bomb *exploded* with a deafening noise.
7. The jazz concert *succeeded* very well.
8. Which girl is Max *dating steadily* now?
9. We should *review* all of the lessons in the book.
10. What are your brothers *interested in* at school?

C. Complete the following sentences by using the proper function words. The meaning is given at the left of each sentence.

1. *excel* — Great leaders stand _____ in times of crisis.
2. *arise* — Should gentlemen stand _____ when a lady enters the room?
3. *represent* — What do the colors of the flag stand _____?
4. *support* — It is important to stand _____ human rights.
5. *last* — How many years will this type of material stand _____?
6. *wait* — The nurses are standing _____ in the emergency room.
7. *excel* — Helen stands _____ in everything she does.
8. *remain firm in face of disapproval* — Don't be afraid of those who are critical; stand _____ them with confidence in yourself.
9. *last* — Mark's new bicycle didn't stand _____ very long.
10. *represent* — What does this political party really stand _____?

D. Complete the following sentences by choosing the correct function word.

1. *over, above* — Is the meeting going _____ as well as we had hoped?
2. *in, on* — The train pulled _____ exactly on time.

3. *through,*   Mr. Hawthorne came _____ in ex-
   around   cellent condition.
4. *down, off*   Attendance at the evening class has
                  fallen _____ considerably.
5. *across, about* How did the accident come _____?
6. *out, through* The doctor says that Mrs. Chester
                  will pull _____.
7. *up, down*   Of all the theories discussed, only one
                  really stood _____.
8. *about, along* Isn't Patricia going to come _____?
9. *up, over*   We're hoping that this crisis will blow
                  _____ and be forgotten.
10. *up, out*   In spite of the earthquake damage,
                  the residents are holding _____ in
                  their determination to remain in
                  their village.
11. *up, out*   Children always seem to grow _____
                  so quickly.
12. *by, for*   The director has asked his assistants
                  to stand _____.
13. *by, to*   Won't you come _____ and visit us
                  next week?
14. *away, under* The brilliant sunset gradually died

                  _____.
15. *out, back*   We arrived just as the bus was pull-
                  ing _____.

Answers to Exercises

LESSON 1

Exercise A.
Page 7

Verbs, in order of appearance: were, delighted, had, admit, were, pleased, was, see, had, choose, was, appear, performed, glowing, astonished, trained, jumping, dancing, pleased, swinging, were, thrilling, was, went

Prepositions, in order of appearance: of, by, to, with, among, in, of, with, in, on, under, to, of, of, around, with, on, above, of, in, of, for

Exercise B. (There are several possible correct answers to each question.)

Exercise C. (There are several possible correct answers to each question.)

LESSON 2

Exercise A.
Page 14

1. The rain put out the huge forest fire. 2. John made up that joke about the talking dog. 3. You should get off the bus at the corner of First and Maple. 4. We are going to look into the disappearance of the money. 5. The entire committee will talk over the proposals. 6. The Parliament carried out the Prime Minister's program. 7. We'll have to put off the dance until next Friday. 8. Margaret came across that quotation in a poem. 9. Boys usually enjoy picking out gifts for others. 10. The chairman's orders brought about a change in policy. 11. Bill often calls up his brother. 12. They turn off the street lights at the same time every morning. 13. Ten young ladies waited on the customers. 14. The county fair was called off because of financial difficulties. 15. Anne ran into a former high school classmate

ast week.   16. We have to put on our best clothes for the
dinner.   17. The Board of Education usually looks over the
class schedule.   18. Please leave out the last ten names on
the list.   19. The nurses brought up the problem of over-
crowding in the hospital.

Exercise B.

1. up   2. on   3. off   4. up   5. over   6. into   7. on
8. off   9. up   10. about   11. out   12. on   13. off   14. out
15. on

Exercise C.

1. ran into   2. take up   3. talk over   4. turned on   5. turn
off   6. make up   7. waiting on   8. came across   9. picked
out   10. left out

Exercise D. (There are several possible correct answers to each question.)

LESSON 3

Exercise A.
Page 23

1. holding it off   2. make it over   3. find it out   4. pointed
them out   5. take it off   6. think them over   7. figure it
out   8. throw it away   9. call them up   10. blew it up
11. put it out   12. do it over   13. looked it over   14. crossed
it out   15. talk it over

Exercise B.

1. The raging fire burned the old wooden building down.
The raging fire burned it down.   2. Constant use will wear
any machine out. Constant use will wear it out.   3. I'd like
to try that blue wool coat on. I'd like to try it on.   4. You
ought to try that radio out before you buy it. You ought to
try it out before you buy it.   5. Mrs. Lowell had her new
dress on last night. Mrs. Lowell had it on last night.   6. The
applicants have to fill several forms out. The applicants have

to fill them out. 7. The workmen put their tools away and left the factory. The workmen put them away and left the factory. 8. Did the firemen put the fire out? Did the firemen put it out? 9. Who threw these perfectly good books away? Who threw them away? 10. Don't take your coat off; it's cold in here. Don't take it off; it's cold in here. 11. Arnold can't figure his algebra problems out. Arnold can't figure them out. 12. You'll have to cross the mistake out. You'll have to cross them out. 13. Why is Mr. Watson holding his decision off? Why is Mr. Watson holding it off? 14. Please do yesterday's assignment over. Please do it over.

Exercise C.

Several answers are permitted for this exercise. One set follows: 1. No, the blue sofa won't go with it. 2. Yes, the class went over them. 3. Yes, Mr. Thompson is going to see about them. 4. No, my daughter doesn't take after me. 5. No, I don't care for it. 6. Yes, the policeman saw through it. 7. Yes, Mr. Porter looked for it at his office. 8. Yes, I came across it in my research. 9. Yes, Miss Glover is going to call on them. 10. No, the union members have not looked into it.

Exercise D.

1. get on, get in 2. get over 3. get through 4. get off 5. get on 6. gotten over 7. get in 8. get through 9. go off 10. get through

Exercise E.

1. Yes, they will look into it. 2. Yes, he has looked it over 3. Yes, you should put it on. 4. Yes, he has put it off 5. Yes, they can put it out. 6. Yes, I put it away. 7. Yes he should try it out. 8. Yes, she is going to call her up 9. Yes, she picked them up. 10. Yes, I picked it out 11. Yes, I will turn it on. 12. Yes, I can turn it off 13. Yes, she took it up. 14. Yes, they should take them off 15. Yes, he takes after him.

LESSON 4

xercise A.
age 31

. live on   2. touch on   3. picking on   4. call on   5. tell
n   6. count on   7. figure on   8. hit on   9. settle on
0. bear on

xercise B.

. run for   2. run into   3. ran over   4. run for   5. ran
ver   6. run across   7. ran into   8. ran against   9. ran
cross

xercise C.

. live on   2. disagree with   3. gone without   4. called on
5. bear on   6. stand for   7. stick to   8. figures on   9. see
o   10. call for   11. get around   12. break into

xercise D.

. of   2. out   3. to   4. up   5. over   6. out   7. over
3. up   9. for   10. against   11. up   12. without   13. for
4. off   15. through   16. on   17. on   18. up   19. out
0. in

xercise E.

1. Yes, I looked it up.   2. Yes, she'll look it over.   3. Yes,
he police have looked into it.   4. Yes, George is looking for
t.   5. Yes, I'm looking at it.   6. Yes, he will look after it.
7. Yes, he got on it.   8. Yes, she will get off it.   9. Yes,
Tom got over it.   10. Yes, we will get through it.   11. Yes,
they can all get in it.   12. Yes, she got around it.

LESSON 5

Exercise A.
Page 40

1. turn out   2. hang up   3. come about   4. showed up
5. go off, blow up   6. let up   7. gave in   8. passed away
9. wore off   10. fall through , break down

Exercise B.

The answers to these questions will vary, but the following verbs should be used in the sentences: 1. break out 2. show up 3. go out 4. get up 5. back up 6. wear off 7. come about 8. break down

Exercise C.

1. let up 2. blow up 3. get up 4. hang up 5. call up
6. brought up 7. pick up 8. show up 9. turned up
10. wakes up 11. made up 12. look up 13. shut up
14. backing up 15. slow up

Exercise D.

1. Please move them over so I can write a letter. 2. He wore them out in less than a month. 3. Steven got off it before it stopped and nearly caused an accident. 4. Turn it on.
5. The ranchers ran them off. 6. Did the public health officials find it out? 7. The students got through it very quickly.
8. The directors will hold it off until next month. 9. I always get in it on the right-hand side. 10. The engineers blew it up to make room for the roadway.

Exercise E.

1. on 2. off, out 3. around 4. up 5. out 6. around
7. on, off 8. up 9. out 10. off, down

LESSON 6

Exercise A.
Page 48

1. The mechanic brought the car over to us after fixing it. The mechanic brought the car back to us after fixing it.
2. Will the factory send the parts over as soon as possible? Will the factory send the parts back as soon as possible?
3. I want to take the photographs over to the studio. I want to take the photographs back to the studio. 4. At 8 p.m., the speaker will go over to the lecture hall. At 8 p.m., the

speaker will go back to the lecture hall.   5. Let's walk over to the house. Let's walk back to the house.   6. The Bakers have invited us over to a party next week. The Bakers have invited us back to a party next week.   7. The box is too heavy; the boys can't carry it over for you. The box is too heavy; the boys can't carry it back for you.

Exercise B.

1. chop it up   2. light them up   3. tear it down . . . fix it up
4. chew it up   5. mixed them up   6. adding them up
7. write it up   8. push them down   9. cutting them down
10. tying them up

LESSON 7

Exercise A.
Page 54

1. The children got excitedly off the bus. The children got off the bus excitedly.   2. The parents heard at last from their son. The parents heard from their son at last.   3. Let's go quickly over the last ten lessons. Let's go over the last ten lessons quickly.   4. My brother doesn't care very much for sports. My brother doesn't care for sports very much.
5. The girls looked hurriedly for their hats and gloves. The girls looked for their hats and gloves hurriedly.   6. Our students keep diligently to their work. Our students keep to their work diligently.   7. This color goes beautifully with black. This color goes with black beautifully.   8. The lecturer touched briefly on several topics. The lecturer touched on several topics briefly.

Exercise B.

1. We came over for a visit.   2. The committee saw to the party arrangements.   3. William often told on his little sister.
4. Those shoes wore out too quickly.   5. Why did they tear the building down?   6. When did you put away your things?
7. I didn't figure out those algebra problems.   8. Did green

apples disagree with everyone? 9. We didn't get around the difficulties. 10. What did his talk bear on? 11. Why did the tourists insist upon getting off the bus? 12. Who ran against Senator Brown? 13. How did the examination turn out? 14. My first impressions wore off.

Exercise C.

1. Why did the secretary throw away those letters which were signed by the president of the company? 2. Will the forest rangers be able to put out the fire raging in the valley? 3. This guide book points out the main facts of early American history. 4. Mrs. Peterson had on a blue and white silk evening dress. 5. Have all of the applicants filled out forms one, two, three, four, and five? 6. Only the best students have been able to figure out this problem in solid geometry. 7. They are using dynamite to blow up the ship that is being used in that movie about the war. 8. A baby's teeth are not strong enough to chew up tough foods like meat and uncooked vegetables. 9. Why did you bring up that difficult, controversial subject at the meeting?

LESSON 8

Exercise A.
Page 60

1. with 2. of 3. with 4. with 5. on 6. under 7. to 8. with 9. on 10. on 11. in 12. to 13. with, in 14. on 15. from 16. of 17. with 18. with 19. for 20. in, with 21. with 22. with 23. for 24. to 25. for

Exercise B.

1. on with, on 2. up on, up 3. up under, up 4. out of, out 5. back to, back 6. along in, along 7. in for, in 8. up with, up 9. on to, on

Exercise C.

1. keep on with 2. come along with 3. fell behind in 4. catch on to 5. fill in for 6. broke in on 7. check up on 8. backed out of 9. bear up under 10. making out in

LESSON 9

Exercise A.
Page 66

1. look up to   2. look down on   3. put up with   4. stand up for   5. came out with   6. come along with   7. do away with   8. look back on   9. play up to   10. get down to

Exercise B.

1. down on   2. forward to   3. on with   4. out for   5. up to   6. back on   7. down on

Exercise C.

1. on   2. of   3. with   4. of   5. to   6. for   7. to   8. with   9. on   10. with   11. with   12. on   13. to   14. with   15. of   16. on   17. to   18. to   19. on   20. for   21. with   22. for

Exercise D.

1. The boys and girls are looking forward to a trip to the beach.   2. Fuller is standing up for the independent policy.   3. My sons go in for stamp collecting and photography.   4. I'm going to do away with the old typewriters.   5. Lawrence fell out with Tom.   6. The Congressman went back on his promise to support a decrease in taxes.   7. Little Billy talked back to his Aunt Dorothy rudely.

LESSON 10

Exercise A.
Page 78

1. called up, call me up   2. looking for, look for   3. broken down, broke down   4. blew up, blew up   5. broke out, broke out   6. make out, make out   7. back up, backed up   8. look up, look me up   9. brush off, brush off   10. call on, call on   11. pick us up, picked up   12. showed her up, showed up   13. take it up, take up   14. mixed up, mix up   15. put on, put on

Exercise B.

1. broken it down   2. broke down   3. broke up   4. broken down   5. break out   6. break the news down   7. broken out   8. broke up   9. broken down   10. broke out

Exercise C.

1. through   2. off   3. on   4. around   5. up   6. on; off   7. around   8. up   9. around   10. off

LESSON 11

Exercise A.
Page 85

1. Why hasn't Richard handed it in?   2. The employer turned him down because of his poor health.   3. The court stenographer wrote it down.   4. How many thieves held it up?   5. Don't make a decision until you think it through.   6. Their first day at the beach tired them out.   7. When is the publishing company going to bring it out?   8. Please turn it in before you leave the classroom.   9. The storm cut it off.   10. Did you manage to cheer them up when you talked to them?   11. The ABC company has bought it out.   12. It isn't always easy to break them in.   13. Let's go down to the ship and see them off.   14. It won't take long to figure them up.   15. The board of directors is going to draw it up.

Exercise B.

1. out   2. out   3. through   4. up   5. out   6. down   7. down   8. in   9. off   10. up

Exercise C.

1. in   2. down   3. up   4. on   5. off   6. out   7. up   8. about   9. up   10. off   11. on   12. out   13. across   14. away

Exercise D.

1. held   2. drawn   3. buy   4. cheered   5. set   6. figure   7. stand   8. mixed   9. let

LESSON 12

Exercise A.
Page 91

1. Why did the press play it down? 2. Joan's dressmaker had to let them down. 3. The children will have to cut them down when school opens. 4. Let's wind them up tonight after dinner. 5. Please ask Harry to hand them out. 6. Why did Dick give it away? 7. William let them down by not accepting the scholarship. 8. No one was able to get it across to the class. 9. When will the owners hand it over to the buyers? 10. Please take it in a little. 11. I'll have to let it out before I can wear it. 12. Who thought it up?

Exercise B.

1. take off 2. hand out, are handing out, handed out 3. hand in 4. gave off, gives off, is giving off 5. giving away 6. taking Della out 7. hand down 8. hand over 9. take in 10. give away 11. give in 12. take up 13. give the money back 14. taken in

Exercise C.

1. Did Paul take out his new girl friend last night? 2. We'll have to touch up the antique chair before we sell it. 3. Have the carpenters used up the floor boards? 4. Did the amateur actors bring off the special performance? 5. Are the doctors carrying over the medical conference? 6. The federal court will hand down the final decision next month. 7. The television reporters played down the unexpected result. 8. The decision was to rule out the last suggestion. 9. Why did they have to cut out the last half?

Exercise D.

1. go over 2. look over 3. carried over 4. talk the problem over 5. got over 6. have everyone in the office over 7. handed his authority over 8. put over 9. do the entire lesson over 10. ran over

LESSON 13

Exercise A.
Page 96

1. made out   2. turn their reports in   3. gave out   4. run it down   5. run his family down   6. passed out   7. gave up   8. clear up   9. run down   10. turn in   11. giving out   12. cleared up   13. break down   14. make out   15. gave up   16. turn out   17. turn out

Exercise B.

1. Yes, I've saved up.   2. Yes, they'll take over immediately.   3. Yes, they kept up.   4. Yes, they're going to close down.   5. Yes, he closed up early today.   6. Yes, he slowed down.   7. Yes, he is going to give up.

Exercise C.

1. cutting down   2. saved up   3. take it over   4. keep it up   5. quiet them down   6. gave up   7. passed out   8. clear it up   9. turns out

Exercise D.

1. turned up   2. turn in   3. turned down   4. turn out   5. turned off   6. turn the radio on   7. turned out   8. turned in   9. turn off   10. turn around

Exercise E.

1. into   2. against   3. into   4. over   5. away   6. across   7. for   8. over   9. off   10. into

LESSON 14

Exercise A.
Page 102

1. down   2. out   3. by   4. over   5. out   6. on   7. over   8. up   9. out   10. in   11. to   12. through   13. by   14. through

Exercise B.

1. go with   2. often go out   3. go back   4. went on with
5. going on   6. went off   7. went over   8. going with
9. go over   10. going in for

Exercise C.

1. out   2. up   3. for   4. up for   5. up   6. by   7. out
8. up to   9. up   10. for

Exercise D.

1. over   2. in   3. through   4. off   5. about   6. through
7. up   8. along   9. over   10. out   11. up   12. by   13. by
14. away   15. out

GLOSSARY

This list includes the two- and three-word verbs used in this book, as well as some that do not appear in the examples and exercises. Normally all these expressions are stressed on the function word, or on the first function word if there are two. Those expressions having the stress on the verb are indicated by asterisks: ***bear on, *call on,** etc.

Page references are to the first occurrence. The symbols used are the following:

sep	separable
+ obj	followed by an object
no obj	not followed by an object
(inf.)	(informal usage)

add up   sep   44   *add*

back down   no obj   *retreat from a position in an argument*

back out   no obj   57   *desert; fail to keep a promise*

back out of   + obj   57   *desert; fail to keep (a promise)*

back up   sep   71   *cause to move backwards; support*

back up   no obj   37   *move backwards*

bawl out   sep   *scold, reprimand* (inf.)

bear down on   + obj   *lean on; browbeat*

*bear on   + obj   28   *be related to, have to do with*

bear up   no obj   57   *endure*

bear up under   + obj   57   *endure*

blow in   no obj   101   *drop in to visit unexpectedly* (inf.)

blow over   no obj   101   *pass without doing harm*

blow up   sep   20   *cause to explode; destroy by explosives*

blow up   no obj   71   *explode; become suddenly angry, lose one's temper* (inf.)

break down   sep   71   *analyze, list the parts of separately*

break down   no obj   37   *cease to function properly;*   71   *become ill to the point of incapacity*

break in   sep   82   *use something new until it is comfortable; use a new machine, such as a car, in a special way at first*

break in   no obj   57   *interrupt*

break in on + obj 57 *interrupt*

break into sep 82 *go into a house or room forcibly; suddenly begin, as laughter, song*

break into + obj 28 *interrupt* (a conversation)

break off sep 89 *end, stop abruptly*

break out no obj 37 *appear, arise, suddenly or violently*

break up sep 44 *break into pieces;* 10-2-A *stop* (a fight); *disperse* (a crowd)

break up no obj 71 *break into small pieces; disperse* (of a group, meeting, *etc.*); *cease associations* (as a married couple, group of friends, *etc.*)

bring about sep 12 *cause to happen*

bring off sep 89 *accomplish* (something difficult *or* unexpected)

bring on sep 89 *cause*

bring out sep 82 *publish, emphasize*

bring over sep 46 *bring*

bring to sep 82 *revive*

bring up sep 12 *raise, care for from childhood*

brush off sep 45 *brush the surface of;* 71 *snub, dismiss without courtesy* (inf.)

brush out sep 45 *brush the inside of*

burn down sep 20 *destroy by burning*

burn up sep 44 *consume by fire*

buy out sep 82 *buy the other person's share of a business*

buy up sep 83 *buy the whole supply of* (a kind of merchandise)

*call for + obj 28 *come to get;* 71 *require* (as a law, recipe, *etc.*)

call off sep 12 *cancel* (something scheduled); 72 *order away* (attacking dogs, troops, *etc.*)

*call on + obj 12 *visit;* 28 *pay a formal visit to; invite to speak in a public meeting;* 72 *ask to serve, etc.; appeal to for help*

call up sep 9 *telephone;* 72 *summon for compulsory military service*

call up no obj 72 *telephone*

calm down sep 94 *become calm; cause to become calm*

calm down no obj 94 *become calm; cause to become calm*

*care for   + obj   20   *like; guard, supervise, maintain, tend*

carry on   sep   12   *continue*

carry on   no obj   72   *continue as before; misbehave* (inf.)

carry on with   + obj   57   *continue*

carry out   sep   12   *fulfill, complete;*   83   *accomplish, perform*

carry over   sep   46   *carry;*   93   *continue on a subsequent page, at a subsequent meeting, etc.*

catch on   no obj   57   *understand* (inf.)

catch up   no obj   57   *cover the distance between oneself and a moving goal*

catch up with   + obj   57   *cover the distance between oneself and*

check out   no obj   57   *leave, pay one's bill*

check out of   + obj   57   *leave* (e.g., *a hotel*)

check up   no obj   57   *investigate*

check up on   + obj   57   *examine, investigate, inspect, verify*

cheer up   sep   72   *cause to become cheerful*

cheer up   no obj   72   *become cheerful*

chew up   sep   44   *chew thoroughly*

chop down   sep   45   *cut* (a tree), *fell*

chop up   sep   44   *chop into small pieces*

clean off   sep   45   *clean the surface of*

clean out   sep   45   *clean the inside of*

clean up   sep   44   *tidy, make neat*

clear off   sep   45   *clear the surface of*

clear out   sep   45   *clear the inside of*

clear out   no obj   *leave* (inf.)

clear up   sep   94   *clarify; tidy*

clear up   no obj   94   *become clear*

close down   sep   94   *close permanently*

close down   no obj   94   *close permanently*

close in   no obj   *encircle and threaten*

close up   sep or no obj   94   *close temporarily*

come about   no obj   37   *happen; in sailing, to turn or change course*

come across   + obj   12   *find accidentally*

come along   no obj   57   *accompany; make progress*

come along with   + obj   57   *accompany; make progress*

come back no obj 46 *return*

*****come by** + obj *find accidentally*

come by no obj 101 *visit someone in his home*

come down with + obj 64 *become ill with*

come out no obj 101 *appear; make a social debut*

come out with + obj 64 *utter, produce*

come to no obj 101 *regain consciousness*

come through no obj 101 *succeed (in spite of difficulties)*

come up to + obj 64 *meet, be equal to*

come up with + obj 64 *utter, produce (unexpectedly or with difficulty)*

come over no obj 45 *come to someone's house, to where someone is*

count in sep 83 *include*

*****count on** + obj 29 *rely on*

count out sep 83 *exclude*

count up sep 44 *calculate;* 83 *count; add to a total*

cross out sep 20 *eliminate*

cut down sep 89 *reduce in quantity*

cut in no obj 57 *interrupt*

cut in on + obj 57 *interrupt*

cut off sep 83 *interrupt; sever, amputate*

cut out sep 89 *eliminate; delete*

cut up sep 44 *cut into small pieces*

die away no obj 101 *fade, diminish*

die down no obj 101 *fade, diminish, grow less intense*

die off/out no obj 101 *disappear, become extinct*

*****disagree with** + obj 29 *cause illness or discomfort to (usually said of food or drink); also used in its literal meaning*

do away with + obj 64 *abolish, eliminate*

do over sep 20 *redo*

do without + obj 29 *deprive oneself of* (something needed)

draw up sep 83 *write, compose* (a document)

dress down sep *reprimand severely*

dress up sep 44 *put clothes on* (someone), *adorn*

dress up no obj *don fancy or unusual clothes*

drive back sep *repulse*

drive back no obj 46 *return by car*

drop in no obj 57 *visit someone casually without previous planning*

drop in at/on + obj 57 *visit casually without previous planning*

drop out no obj 37 *abandon some organized activity;* 57 *leave, quit*

drop out of + obj 57 *leave (an activity), quit*

drop over no obj 45 *visit someone casually* (inf.)

dust out sep 45 *dust the inside of*

eat up sep 44 *eat completely*

face up to + obj 64 *acknowledge (something unpleasant or difficult)*

fall back on + obj 64 *use for emergency purposes*

fall behind no obj 57 *lag; not progress at the required pace*

fall behind in + obj 57 *lag; not progress at the required pace in*

fall off no obj 101 *decrease; lose weight*

fall out with + obj 64 *quarrel with*

fall through no obj 37 *fail, not be accomplished*

feel up to + obj 64 *feel one has the strength or ability to do* (something)

*****figure on** + obj 29 *estimate; expect*

figure out sep 20 *interpret, understand*

figure up sep 83 *compute*

fill in sep *complete* (a printed form)

fill in no obj 57 *substitute*

fill in for + obj 57 *substitute for*

fill out sep 20 *complete* (a printed form)

fill up sep 44 *fill completely* (a container)

find out sep 20 *discover*

find out no obj 38 *learn*

fix up sep 44 *repair; arrange in suitable manner*

fly back no obj 46 *return by air*

fly over no obj 45 *fly to where someone is*

get across sep 89 *cause to be understood*

get ahead no obj 58 *make progress*

get ahead of + obj 58 *surpass; beat*

get along no obj 58 *have a friendly relationship*

get along with + obj 58 *have a friendly relationship with*

get around + obj   29   *evade, avoid*

get around no obj   72   *circulate, move about (inf.)*

get away no obj   58   *escape*

get away with + obj   64   *do* (something wrong) *without being caught or punished*

get by no obj   58   *manage, either just barely or with a minimum of effort*

get by with + obj   58   *manage with difficulty; manage with a minimum of effort*

get down to + obj   64   *become serious about; (at last) consider*

get in + obj   20   *enter* (a vehicle, enclosed space)

get in no obj   38   *enter*

get off sep   73   *send, dispatch; succeed in removing*

get off + obj   12   *descend from, leave (e.g., a vehicle)*

get off no obj   38   *descend from, leave (e.g., a vehicle)*

get on sep   73   *don, put on*

get on no obj   38   *enter (e.g., a vehicle); mount (a horse, etc.)*

get on + obj   12   *enter* (a vehicle);   73   *mount*

get on/along no obj   73   *progress; be compatible*

get on/along with + obj   73   *be compatible with*

get on with + obj   *proceed with* (an activity)

get over + obj   20   *recover from* (a disease, injury, *etc.*)

get through + obj   20   *finish; make one's way through*

get through no obj   38   *finish; make one's way through*

get through (with) + obj   73   *terminate; finish*

get up sep   73   *cause to rise*

get up no obj   37   *rise* (from bed, from a sitting or lying position)

give away sep   83   *give (indiscriminately, as something one no longer wants); betray (a secret, a trust)*

give back sep   46   *return* (something taken or borrowed)

give in no obj   37   *surrender, stop resisting*

give off sep   89   *emit (e.g., rays, a smell, etc.)*

give out sep   94   *distribute, announce*

give out no obj   94   *become exhausted (inf.)*

give up sep   94   *surrender something*

give up no obj   94   *surrender; fail to finish*

go back no obj   46   *return*

go back on + obj 64 *desert; fail to keep* (a promise)

***go for** + obj *like a great deal* (inf.)

go in for + obj 64 *be interested in, participate in* (inf.)

go off no obj 37 *explode* (as fireworks)

go on no obj 36 *happen;* 58 *continue*

go on with + obj 58 *continue*

go out no obj 37 *stop burning* (said of a fire or a light);
also used literally, *leave one's residence*

go over + obj 20 *review*

go over no obj 46 *go;* 101 *succeed*

go through with + obj 64 *persevere, complete in spite of
difficulties*

***go with** + obj 20 *harmonize with;* 29 *look pleasing to-
gether* (of colors, furniture, clothing, *etc.*); *accompany a
person of the opposite sex in public, for courtship*

go without + obj 29 *abstain from* (something needed)

grow up no obj 101 *mature*

hand down sep 89 *deliver, pronounce formally* (in
court); *leave as an inheritance*

hand in sep 83 *submit, present*

hand out sep 89 *distribute publicly*

hand over sep 89 *yield control of*

hang around + obj 29 *remain idly in the vicinity of*
(inf.)

hang around no obj 73 *remain idly, dawdle* (inf.)

hang up sep 37 *suspend*

hang up no obj 37 *replace a telephone receiver on its
hook*

have on sep 20 *be dressed in*

have over sep 83 *entertain someone informally at one's
home*

***hear from** + obj 20 *receive a communication from*

***hear of** + obj 29 *learn about, often accidentally*

***hit on** + obj 29 *discover accidentally*

hold off sep 20 *delay; restrain*

hold on no obj 58 *grasp tightly;* 73 *support oneself
by grasping with the hands; persevere; wait while telephoning* (inf.)

hold on to + obj 58 *grasp tightly*

hold out no obj 58 *continue to resist;* 101 *persevere; persist*

hold out against + obj 58 *resist*

hold up sep 83 *delay; rob, threatening the victim with a weapon*

invite over sep 46 *ask someone to visit* (inf.)

keep at + obj *persevere at* (an activity)

keep on no obj 58 *continue*

keep on with + obj 58 *continue*

*****keep to** + obj 29 *persist in, continue*

keep up sep 94 *continue, keep the same pace*

keep up no obj 58 *maintain the required pace or standard;* 94 *continue*

keep up with + obj 58 *maintain the pace of*

lay in sep *equip one's household with, usually in anticipation of future needs*

leave out sep 18 *omit*

let down sep 89 *disappoint; make longer* (in sewing)

let out sep 89 *release from confinement; make larger* (in sewing)

let up no obj 37 *diminish in intensity*

lie down no obj 36 *recline*

lie down on + obj 64 *evade, fail to do* (one's duty toward)

light up sep 44 *light, illuminate thoroughly*

live down sep *live in such a way as to cause* (something shameful in one's past) *to be forgiven*

*****live on** + obj 29 *sustain or support oneself by means of*

live up to + obj 64 *maintain the standard demanded by*

look after + obj 29 *take care of*

look back on + obj 64 *remember nostalgically*

look down on + obj 64 *feel superior to, scorn*

*****look for** + obj 20 *seek*

look forward to + obj 64 *anticipate (usually with pleasure)*

look into + obj 10 *investigate*

look on no obj *be a spectator*

look over sep 19 *examine*

look up sep 19 *seek* (information) *in a reference book;* 10-4 *locate and visit*

look up to + obj 64 *respect, admire* (someone)

make out sep 74 *understand, with difficulty; decipher;*
  94 *write a check, document, etc.*

make out no obj 58 *progress; succeed*

make out in/with + obj 58 *progress; succeed*

make over sep 20 *remake*

make up sep 12 *invent, compose;* 69 *write; complete*
  what was missed; apply cosmetics

make up no obj *become reconciled*

make up for + obj 64 *compensate for*

mix up sep 44 *mingle thoroughly;* 74 *confuse*

move over sep 37 *move* (something) *to the side*

move over no obj 36 *move to the side*

pan out no obj 83 *turn out well, be successful* (inf.)

pass away no obj 37 *die*

pass out sep 95 *distribute*

pass out no obj 95 *become unconscious*

pass up sep *not take advantage of, as an opportunity*

pass on sep 69 *transmit*

*pass on + obj 69 *make a decision* (said of a governing
  body)

pass on no obj 69 *die*

pay back sep 46 *repay*

pay off sep *discharge a debt completely; give someone his*
  final pay at the end of a job

*pick on + obj 29 *tease, bully, tyrannize, usually in petty*
  but humiliating ways

pick out sep 12 *select*

pick up sep 20 *take or lift with the hands or fingers;*
  74 *come to meet and escort* (someone); *learn, casually*
  and without particular effort; initiate an association with
  someone in public, often not under respectable circum-
  stances

pick up no obj 74 *grow, increase* (inf.)

play down sep 89 *minimize* (inf.)

play up sep *emphasize* (inf.)

play up to + obj 64 *flatter for personal advantage*

point out sep 20 *indicate*

pull down sep 45 *pull* (something) *in a downward direc-*
  tion; raze (a structure)

pull in no obj 101 *arrive (of a vehicle)*

pull out no obj 101 *depart (of a vehicle)*

pull through no obj 101 *survive (barely)*

push down sep 45 *push in a downward direction*

put across sep 83 *cause* (an idea or suggestion) *to be understood or accepted*

put away sep 20 *store; put in its proper place*

put off sep 12 *postpone*

put on sep 12 *dress in;* 82 *deceive or fool*

put out sep 12 *extinguish; inconvenience* (someone)

put up sep *preserve* (food *in sealed containers*); *receive as an overnight guest*

put up with + obj 64 *tolerate*

quiet down sep or no obj 94 *be quiet; cause to be quiet*

read up on + obj 65 *search out information* (on a topic) *for some special purpose*

ride over no obj 45 *ride to where someone is*

ring up sep *telephone* (chiefly British)

rinse off sep 45 *rinse the surface of*

rinse out sep 45 *rinse the inside of*

rule out sep 89 *eliminate*

run across + obj 29 *find or meet accidentally*

run against + obj 29 *compete against in an election*

run away no obj 36 *escape;* 58 *leave;* 75 *leave quickly without permission or authorization*

run away from + obj 58 *leave; escape from*

run down sep 95 *trace; disparage; hit with a vehicle*

run down no obj 95 *slowly lose power so as to stop functioning* (e.g., as a watch)

*__run for__ + obj 29 *campaign for* (an elective office)

run into + obj 10 *meet by accident*

run off sep 37 *cause to depart;* 75 *drive away; reproduce* (copies of something) *mechanically*

run off no obj 36 *depart running;* 75 *drain (of water)*

run out of + obj 65 *not have any more of* (something)

save up sep or no obj 94 *accumulate*

*__see about__ + obj 20 *consider, arrange*

see off sep 83 *accompany someone to the beginning of a trip, e.g., to a ship, or a train*

*see to   + obj   29   *arrange, supervise, take responsibility for*
    for
see through   sep   83   *complete, in spite of difficulties*
sell out   sep or no obj   94   *sell the ownership* (of a business)
    ness)
send back   sep   46   *send to a place where formerly located*
send over   sep   46   *send to where someone is*
set up   sep   83   *arrange*
*settle on   + obj   29   *decide on, choose, after a period of
    uncertainty*
settle up   no obj   *pay one's bills or debts*
show off   sep   *exhibit ostentatiously*
show off   no obj   *boast by words or actions*
show up   sep   75   *prove* (someone) *to be wrong, dishonest, etc.* (inf.)
    honest, etc. (inf.)
show up   no obj   37   *arrive, appear unexpectly or inopportunely* (inf.)
    tunely (inf.)
shut off   sep   *cause to cease functioning* (*e.g.,* a motor,
    water pipe)
shut up   sep   37   *cause to become silent* (*very informal,
    to be avoided*)
shut up   no obj   37   *stop talking* (*an impolite, rather vulgar expression*)
    gar expression)
slow down   sep or no obj   94   *go more slowly*
slow up   sep   37   *cause to move more slowly*
slow up   no obj   36   *reduce speed*
spell out   sep   83   *enumerate, state, in detail*
stand by   no obj   101   *wait, be prepared to assist*
*stand for   + obj   29   *represent; permit, endure; campaign
    for* (an elective office, *in Britain*)
stand out   no obj   101   *be noticeable, excel*
stand up   sep   75   *fail to keep an appointment with* (inf.)
stand up   no obj   36   *stand, rise from a sitting position;*
    101   *last, endure*
stand up for   + obj   65   *support, defend*
stand up to   + obj   65   *resist, remain firm in the face of*
    (opposition or disapproval)
stay over   no obj   46   *remain at someone's house overnight, or longer*
    night, or longer
step aside   no obj   36   *move to one side*

*stick to + obj 29 *persist, persevere*
stick up for + obj 65 *support, defend*
sweep out sep 45 *sweep the inside of*
*take after + obj 20 *resemble* (as a child a parent)
take back sep 46 *return; retract a statement*
take down sep 45 *remove* (something from a high position); *write from dictation*
take in sep 89 *understand* (something); *fool, deceive* (someone); *make smaller* (in sewing)
take off sep 20 *remove* (as clothes); *take* (an amount of time) *as leave*
take off no obj 76 *leave the ground* (of aircraft); *leave, or not report for, work*
take over sep 46 *take;* 94 *assume command of*
take over no obj 94 *assume command*
take out sep 89 *accompany someone socially; remove*
take up sep 12 *begin to study, prepare for a career in;* 76 *consider at a public meeting, discuss; shorten* (a garment)
talk back no obj 58 *answer impolitely*
talk back to + obj 58 *answer impolitely*
talk over + obj 10 *discuss*
tear down sep 45 *destroy* (a structure)
tear up sep 44 *tear into small pieces*
tell off sep *scold, reprimand* (inf.)
*tell on + obj 29 *report* (a child's) *misbehavior to someone in authority*
think over sep 20 *consider*
think through sep 83 *consider something from beginning to end*
think up sep 89 *create, invent*
throw away sep 20 *discard*
throw over sep *reject* (a suitor)
throw up no obj *vomit* (inf.)
tie up sep 44 *tie securely or tight*
tire out sep 83 *cause to be exhausted*
*touch on + obj 29 *mention briefly in speech or writing*
touch up sep 89 *repair, add finishing touches to*
try on sep 20 *put on* (a garment) *to verify the fit*

try out   sep   20   *test, use experimentally*
turn around   no obj   36   *turn so that one is facing an-*
    other direction
turn down   sep   83   *refuse; lower the volume* (of a radio,
    etc.)
turn in   sep   95   *submit; deliver*
turn in   no obj   95   *go to bed* (inf.)
turn into   + obj   49   *become, be transformed into*
turn off   sep   12   *stop the operation of* (a machine, *etc.*)
turn on   + obj   attack unexpectedly
turn on   sep   10   *start the operation of* (a machine, *etc.*)
turn out   sep   76   *produce (serially); dismiss* (someone
    from the place where he usually lives), *force into exile;*
    95   *extinguish* (a light)
turn out   no obj   37   *succeed;*   95   *come, appear, as at a*
    public meeting
turn up   sep   83   *discover, find* (inf.)
turn up   no obj   *arrive, be found, unexpectedly* (inf.)
use up   sep   89   *use all of*
wait on   + obj   10   serve
wait up   no obj   58   *remain awake in anticipation of*
    something
wait up for   + obj   58   *not go to bed while waiting for*
wake up   no obj   36   *awaken*
walk back   no obj   46   *return on foot to where one was*
walk over   no obj   45   *walk to where someone is*
wash off   sep   45   *wash the surface of*
wash out   sep   45   *wash the inside of*
wash out   no obj   *fade or disappear from washing* (as
    color, spots on fabric, *etc.*)
wash up   sep   44   *wash thoroughly, wash all the pieces of*
watch out   no obj   58   *be careful*
watch out for   + obj   58   *be careful of*
wear off   no obj   37   *fade, disappear through use or time*
wear out   sep   20   *use* (something) *until no longer usable;*
    tire greatly, exhaust the strength of
wear out   no obj   38   *become unusable through use;*   76
    become used up, no longer serviceable
wind up   sep   89   *finish* (inf.); *tighten the spring of a*
    timepiece or similar machine

wipe off   sep   45   *wipe the surface of*

wipe out   sep   45   *wipe the inside of; decimate, slaughter all living members of* (a group, army, *etc.*)

work out   sep   94   *solve*

work out   no obj   94   *be successful*

write down   sep   83   *record*

write out   sep   83   *write down every detail of, spell out*

write up   sep   44   *compose, prepare* (a report, or similar document)